# Wandering in Cornwall
## Mystery, Mirth and Transformation
## in the Land of Ancient Celts

Dear Rick & Diane —
Never stop wandering!
Hugs,
Lynne
(pgs. 51 & 181 ☺)

Cornish countryside with Saint Michael's Mount in the background

# WANDERING IN CORNWALL
## MYSTERY, MIRTH AND TRANSFORMATION
## IN THE LAND OF ANCIENT CELTS

Edited by
Joanna Biggar &
Linda Watanabe McFerrin

Wanderland Writers
Oakland, California

For permission to print essays in this volume, grateful acknowledgement is made to the holders of copyright named on pages 214–223.

Photographs
*Front cover:* © JM Shubin
*Back cover:* Linda and Joanna ©Hugh Biggar
Cornish landscape © JM Shubin
*Interior photos:*
© Unity Barry: page 42
© Jonas Bengtsson (Wikimedia): page 108
© Tony Farrell: page 38
© Peter Gudella (Shutterstock): page 28
© Kitty Hughes: pages 68, 138
© Piotr Kamionka (123RF): page xvi
© Laurie McAndish King: pages 20, 116, 122, 192, 210
© Ethel Mussen: page 96
© MJ Pramik: page 130
© Lynne Rutan: page 50
© JM Shubin: pages ii, vi, xiii, 76, 84, 90, 104, 146, 152, 158, 166, 180, 188, 202
© Maryly Snow: page 172
© Helen Wilkinson (Wikimedia): page 12
Public domain: pages 8, 58

Cover design, interior design, map and photo illustrations by JM Shubin, Shubin Design (www.shubindesign.com)
Typefaces: Sabon and Garamond

Printing: Lowry McFerrin,
ProForma Mactec Solutions (lowry.mcferrin@proforma.com)

CATALOGING DATA:
Wandering in Cornwall: Mystery, Mirth and Transformation in the Land of Ancient Celts
Edited by Linda Watanabe McFerrin and Joanna Biggar
ISBN: 978-0-9964390-1-5

First Printing 2015
Printed in the United States of America

To our travel and writing companions—those lost and those still with us—
whose stories take us further than we would normally go ...
and bring us home.

# CONTENTS

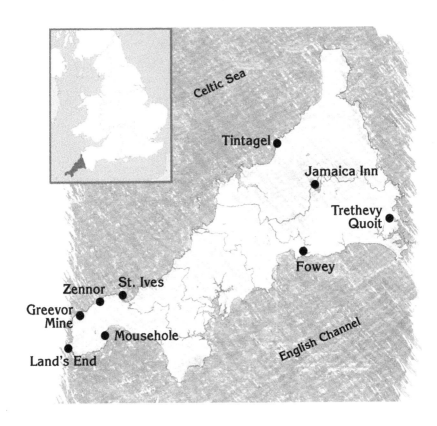

Cornwall juts out from England's extreme southwest

# INTRODUCTION

*"Words, English, English words, are full of echoes, memories, associations naturally that have been out and about on people's lips, in houses, in fields for centuries."*
—Virginia Woolf, recorded speaking "On Craftsmanship," for the BBC

These most English of words greeted us at a display in the British Library in London, site of the London Book Festival's ceremonial gathering, during which our most recent Wanderland Writers anthology, *Wandering in Paris: Luminaries and Love in the City of Light* was awarded First Place in its category. We were unable to attend. But there we were, a year later, in England on yet another Wanderland Writers adventure, this time to Cornwall, a rich literary landscape, birthplace of Arthurian legend, setting for the *chansons de geste*, and home over the ensuing centuries to hosts of writers, painters, sculptors, photographers, potters and other artists. The British Library—with words, manuscripts and more inspiration from sources as diverse as the *Magna Carta*, Shakespeare's *Folios*, Charlotte Brontë's *Jane Eyre*, and Lewis Carroll's *Alice in Wonderland*—seemed a most fitting place to begin our English journey and gather inspiration.

We did find inspiration—plenty of it—but we also came upon a cautionary tale. As we contemplated pages from a stunning *Gutenberg Bible*, we were struck by the fate of Johannes Gutenberg after his publishing breakthrough: "*Gutenberg was less successful as a businessman than as an innovator, and his business dissolved shortly after completion of the* Bible."

Oh dear, if the most popular book ever written did not keep its publisher afloat, what hope could there be for the industry? We concluded that publishing at its best is always a labor of love, yet there we were again, foolishly smitten and determined to write, edit and publish another anthology. In it we present stories about everything from pasties to pixies, from clotted cream to castles. We have gathered tales that reflect the landscape as our writers experienced it while they wandered the length and breadth of Cornwall by car, by bike, by kayak and on foot, and wrote to their heart's content in the literary terrain that inspired the works of the French *trouvères*, Virginia Woolf, Daphne du Maurier, Agatha Christie, Thomas Hardy and more.

Some or our writers descended into the very bowels of the earth as Tom, Kitty and MJ did in their stories of Cornish mining, while others let their imaginations take flight. Some were drawn to water, some to the very stones that form the bedrock of this world. In addition to the dramatic landscape of Cornwall, from rocky cliffs dropping into the sea to stone-strewn moors, we also drew inspiration from the many great writers who had come before and left their mark on this rugged peninsula. It was hard not to fall under their spell, from the earliest versions of Arthurian legend to Thomas Hardy, D.H. Lawrence, and the ubiquitous Daphne du Maurier, whose transformations of real landmarks into haunting works of fiction—the manor house of Menabilly, the Jamaica Inn, Frenchman's Creek near Fowey—shadowed us at every turn.

And visible from the vantage point of our digs on the hilltop of Tregenna Castle, the lighthouse on Godvrey Island, transformed by Virginia Woolf into her own in *To the Lighthouse*, inspired us daily and was our beacon, a reminder that a book, a story, a poem can transport us, can take us someplace lasting, can spirit us away, can bring us safely home.

For our readers, we hope these stories provide a delightful introduction to Cornwall and the vicinity, though we feel that Virginia Woolf says it best and should also get the last word.

*... I could fill pages remembering one thing after another. All together made the summer at St. Ives the best beginning to life imaginable.*

—Virginia Woolf, *Moments of Being*

—Linda Watanabe McFerrin and Joanna Biggar
Oakland, California and Aix-en-Provence, France

The lighthouse on Godvrey Island

# FOREWORD

Cornwall, its peninsula trailing west from Britain's southern shires like an afterthought, has ever been a place apart. In the sixth century it was the last refuge of Celtic tribes who were driven to land's end by Saxon invaders. In the ninth century their descendants would be forced to bow to Anglo-Saxon overlords, but for a thousand years they would keep their own language and culture as part of England's Celtic Fringe. Separate. Distinct. Distant. Even today Cornwall is a world away from the frenetic madness that is London, so far away that those who come here do not stumble upon it by chance. When they come, it is with a purpose.

For this is a land of quests, of dark legends, mystery, and heartbreaking romance. Cornwall is where Tristan and Iseult shared a hopeless love; where Uther's lust for Ygraine led to Arthur's mythical birth; where Merlin was enchanted and entombed by Nimue. Its headlands and bays have been prowled by Conan Doyle's Holmes, by Winston Graham's Poldark, by Daphne du Maurier's gothic heroines, and by Susan Cooper's child heroes who, like Arthur, continue valiantly to lead the forces of light against a threatening darkness.

That stark contrast between darkness and light captures, for me, the essence of Cornwall: white sea foam splashing on brooding granite rocks, castle ruins silhouetted against a milky sky, sun-washed megaliths planted on a dark moor, and whitewashed stone cottages with windows and doors trimmed boldly in black. There is beauty in the contrast, perhaps because shadow is such an effective tool for defining the light, or perhaps because we recognize in that play of light and dark the dual elements of human nature.

Cornwall's history, too, and the livelihoods of its people have been veined with darkness. For generations they braved the depths of the earth in search of tin or set out in the pre-dawn gloom to work the sea for fish. The tin mines are closed now, the skeletal remains of their engine houses adding to the savage beauty of the landscape. The fishing industry lingers on, however, for Cornwall is bounded on three sides by the sea with so many coves and inlets one imagines that its coastline was carved with a giant spoon.

That rugged shore now draws artists, writers and tourists to its pretty harbor towns. From Polperro to Penzance, from St. Ives to Port Isaac, they come in search of—something. Sometimes they find what they are looking for. Sometimes they find something else. I went looking for Arthur's Tintagel, and I found a stark beauty I should have expected yet hadn't imagined. I found, too, the kernel of a dream that would take half a lifetime to blossom. That was thirty years ago, and although I have returned to Britain many times since, my road has never again led me across the River Tamar. Perhaps now it is time to go back, to revisit Tintagel and Polperro, and to look once again for inspiration in the darkness and the light of Cornwall.

—Patricia Bracewell
*Author of Shadow on the Crown* and *The Price of Blood*

Commemorative Flanders poppies

# A QUESTION OF COURAGE

*Linda Watanabe Mcferrin*

The poppies tumble from the Tower of London in a great flood of scarlet. Ceramic-hard and bright, they spread, individually anchored by willing hands until they fill the moat that surrounds the Tower in an ever-widening ocean of red: one flower for each of the 888,246 British and Colonial lives lost in World War I. The installation created by artists Paul Cummins and Tom Piper commemorates the one-hundredth anniversary of a war that began on July 28, 1914, and took over sixteen million lives by the time it ended more than four years later. Standing with Paula, Jholeen and Paula's husband, Mark, I can't take my eyes off the volunteers as they bend and kneel, planting each flower with a careful reverence, their obeisance mirroring my own heart's genuflections.

It's been only a month since I lost my younger sister in a fatal car crash, and although I'm here in England to teach, to write, to travel and explore and guide a group of writers in the production of yet another anthology, I feel weak, as insubstantial as a poppy petal, something that the strong September wind can blow away.

Was it a mistake to come here? My grandfather was Welsh. I spent years as a little girl in Britain. My sister, Amelia, was born in England, in Wiltshire, and though I have returned to this country many times since

1

those early days and have written about the British Isles often over the years, on this occasion everything is different. I'm headed for Cornwall with its ports and beaches, its moors and seaside villages and towns, but I have a feeling most of the terrain I'll be traversing is an interior landscape, one creased with sorrow.

Even the train journey from London's Paddington Station to St. Ives is disturbing. Someone has thrown himself upon the tracks. I meditate on the kind of misery that leads a person to such despair, and reflect. Novels filled with suicides—including one that I've written—come to mind as do events in my life: the kind of wrenching drama best found in books but all too often part of a world that cannot be conveniently closed or tucked away on a bookcase and forgotten.

The track is cleared. The trains move on. The fairytale landscapes of my childhood scroll past the windows of the carriage. These are the settings for stories in which the sun is forever coming out from behind the clouds and Sally and Dick and Jane are always closing up their big black umbrellas and Puff-the-cat and Spot-the-dog are prancing out to play. The day is bright, the weather fine, but it's as if I have a dark cloud circling around my head. My travel companions try to chat with me, and I do my best to interact, but my mind is elsewhere.

Reading, Taunton, Exeter, Exmouth, Torquay, Plymouth, St. Austell, Truro, St. Erth—our destination, the Cornish coast, mocks me. St. Ives is a beautiful town perched on a hill above the sea with literally boatloads of flowers and the sunlight streaming down all around it. Tregenna Castle, almost a cliché in its picture-perfectness, sits atop a green hill, as castles should, with lawns and lodges and cottages and gardens and vistas that embrace the whole surround. The very cheerfulness fuels my sense of isolation.

In the days that follow, I'm dreadful company. Gloom ghosts my every step. In Fowey, where Daphne du Maurier, a favorite author of my

2

adolescence, lived and wrote, I dawdle in churchyards. On Bodmin Moor, home of that legendary den of smugglers, the Jamaica Inn, I eagerly turn my face into the chapping winds. At Tintagel, where it is supposed that King Arthur was illicitly conceived on a dark and stormy night, I linger on the disintegrating stairs that climb the cliffs and squint morosely out at the glinting, sun-bossed sea. I can't bear the thought of the dank tin mines.

Although we are a good-sized tribe of writers and wanderers, much of the time I am without companions. In St. Ives, abandoned, I visit the little pubs alone, chat with the locals, my stranger status allowing me an entrée into conversations where truths are told with little thought of consequences. In solitary fashion I haunt the town—the bookstore, the markets, the teashops—scurrying down the hill, over the cobbled streets. At night I cannot sleep.

St. Ives worms its way into my solitude. In spite of the current kite-bright weather the town has something flinty about it, hard and tough as the crust on the moon-shaped pasties that I tuck into whenever I find them. This is, after all, a hardscrabble place and, like me, a little scarred. Here in Cornwall, where livelihoods have been fished from wrecking seas and scratched from wretched mines, life pulls no punches.

I think it is this bleak Hardy-esque reality, the anniversary of a great war and the shadow of my recent loss that draws me to ask Tony Farrell to tell me more about the effect of conflict on the Cornish Coast. Tony, a handsome Cornishman and a poet to boot, was Head of English at St. Ives School and leads archeological tours and walks around St. Ives and West Penwith, also known as the Land's End Peninsula. We meet at the Fishermen's Lodges located in the harbor area, between Smeaton's pier and Porthminster Beach. Built for the fisherman of St. Ives, only three lodges remain: The Rose, The Shore Shelter and The Shamrock. Originally built on the sand, two were moved to their current site on firmer ground

3

through a bequest from the estate of Sir Edward Hain, a St. Ives native and wealthy shipping magnate whose only son died tragically in 1915 in Gallipoli during the Dardanelle's campaign. Sir Edward died just two years after.

For that and other reasons, this seems an appropriate meeting place. The Rose is cozy, clean, well swept and tended to by the fishermen themselves who still congregate around the pot belly stove, breeze in to chat and exchange news, or pause to wind the clock. The walls of the lodge are covered with old photographs—a kind of unofficial maritime museum. There's a story in each of the photos tacked up around us, and that is perfect, because the questions I have for Tony center around these people, their ups and—as seems most appropriate to me at this time in my own life—their downs.

Tony complies. He talks about the Great War—that war to end all wars—and the wars that followed, about pilchards and tin and bad weather and the economy and the rigors of wage earning in a place where every comfort is hard won. His own story is sculpted from this country. His grandfather, William Trevorrow Farrell, fought in WWI as did his grandfather's brother. William's brother went to Mesopotamia and William went to Palestine, where he was wounded in Beersheba and nearly died. According to Tony, his grandfather spent three days on a camel, losing blood, but eventually survived only to be sent to another front where he was wounded again.

William's son—Tony's father—also fought in a war—WWII. "I owe my existence to Hitler," says Tony. His uncle Tommy, who served in that war as well, was wounded and sent—semi-paralyzed—to convalesce in a facility in Exeter. On a visit to see his brother, Tony's father met his future wife, Tony's mother. She, too, was in recovery there, having lost the fingers on her right hand in an explosion at the munitions factory at which she'd been working. "For me the war was just part of the world," confesses Tony. "We didn't really talk about it."

4

But on this day we are talking about it, and I am glad. We're talking truth here, about a more personal form of history: the trials that test us and sometimes yield great revelations, the hard times that make heroes. And so it goes as we continue the conversation in the little Fisherman's Lodge, the stories of difficult times, great disasters, wars fought, men lost, ships sunk, and uncertain futures spooling out around us.

Later, before we move on to some of the great archeological sites, to the Celtic fields and structures where Tony's knowledge and professional expertise will bestow a very different form of enlightenment, we head up to Barnoon Cemetery. Located in St. Ives, on a hill above Porthmeor Beach, it's really here that my journey with Tony ends, even as the actual tour begins. The little cemetery, full of wildflowers and sun-bleached headstones, is unkempt in the most attractive of ways. Of course it is. How can I, the moody writer of zombie tales, not find a place here? There are ancient gravesites and newer ones, many for the men and women who served in the Royal Navy Reserve, the Royal Defense Corps, the Women's Royal Navy Service, the Mercantile Marine, the H.M. Coastguard, the Duke of Cornwall's Light Infantry, the Royal Garrison Artillery, the Royal Air Force and so on. This is no dreary churchyard, however. The site is cheerful, the sea below as bright as a blue eye, the wind brisk and refreshing, the ghosts tossed like thin white curtains in a clarifying way. Tony speaks proudly of the men and women buried here. I feel as comfortable as I did in the Fishermen's Lodges, and greatly comforted too. I consider the living and the dead, but mostly I consider the way the living deal with those who've passed, and I realize that it's really not about the wars or the losses.

The world is crushing and, first or last, we all will fall. But what I've learned here is something about the spirit, how the important thing is how we deal with devastation. It's something Tony and the people hereabouts seemed to know through tough experience—how to soldier on. I love this about the Cornish, the British, my friends in London, many of my friends at home, my remaining family members and my sister, when she was still alive: I love the way their spirits do not falter when they are tasked to perform ... or if they do, the way they rise above it. I hope it's something I'll remember in the days and years to come. There is no war to end all wars, but there is bravery. There is courage.

Virginia Woolf

# POCKETS FULL OF STONES
*Antoinette Constable*

*For Virginia Woolf, 1882-1941*

In the fairy tale, the resourceful older boy
protects his younger sister.
When the path in the woods narrows
to the width of a shoe, he turns around
to make sure she isn't far behind.
And though they often quarrel,
they care for each other
and the ballast they gathered
in their pockets
saves them, gleaming
like grounded fireflies
all the way home.

Now a famous writer, she feels worthless,
as if she's lost
everything of value. There's no one to help.
She's alone against the pieces of her tearing mind

in the country dusk with stars like moths on a glass dome
reflecting her older brother's face. She kneels
in her long skirt and with lovely hands unused to it,
scratches the river bank and breaks her nails
uprooting stones she holds close
for the brief reassurance of their solidity.
More. She must have
more stones.

Lips tight over her teeth, oblivious
to the stains on her skirt, she stores them
reflexively, like change for the ferry,
in her cardigan pockets,
now grotesque, drooping over
her upper thighs. When she straightens,
in the night above she sees
millions of black-draped cameras trained on her.
She remembers her girlhood dread of being home
alone with one of her older brothers.

To escape, she must go down,
down into the stream.
She enters the river, fully dressed,
her shoes gurgling at first,
coming off at the heels as she slides on algae,
bends back then forward at the waist
for balance, fingers above the waves.
Now the wet hem of her dress
wraps itself, cool on her calves and knees
like freshly rinsed towels.

She hesitates, but overhead
the cameras flash, invaders on the river.
Shaking, she takes more steps
into the darkly rolling wash.

Her raised arms lower into the current
to reach her ballast hold. Amazed
she finds her arms so heavy in their sleeves,
stiffening like plaster bandages—her empty belly
hard, her keen heart turning murderously to stone.

She leans face-down into the broad, shifting hammock
for a shawl, for a wall, for a door, for a bolt
to lock, to guarantee a girl's inviolate safety
in a room of her own.

Geevor Mine

# MINING MEMORIES
*Thomas Harrell*


One hundred feet down in the dark, I crouched to feel my way through
an abandoned mining tunnel. It was barely as wide as my shoulders, and
sometimes not even that. As I prayed silently to gods known and unknown,
and the Cornish imps called piskies for good measure, the whole time I
was thinking, "This one's for you, Mom."

If I could build a time machine and take us back to the spring of
1977, you would find my mother and me glued to the couch on Sunday
nights watching the BBC production of *Poldark*, an absurdly addictive
costume drama set in 1780s Cornwall among the copper and tin mines
that covered the land like spider webs. With my father starting a new job
out of town and my brother newly away to college, it was just the two
of us living in Arizona in the months before I finished high school. And
what better way to bond than over a weekly dose of love, betrayal,
revenge, and lives lost and fortunes won among the Cornish mines, all
dressed in the respectability of period costumes and British accents?

In those days you did not stream video, binge watch Netflix, or
program a DVR. There were not hundreds of cable stations; with rabbit
ears, our leviathan of a television boasted maybe six channels. No, my
mom and I had to wait impatiently week after week for Alistair Cook to

feed our addiction. The characters of *Poldark*—including Ross Poldark, the eponymous hero returned to Cornwall from war in the rebellious colonies to find his former love Elizabeth engaged to his cousin; Ross's servant turned wife, Demelza; and a memorable host of others—became almost a surrogate family in those months. Sunday nights were a magic carpet ride to eighteenth-century Cornwall.

Winston Graham wrote the series of books on which *Poldark* was based, and he subtitled the books, *Novels of Cornwall*. His Cornwall is a hard place, a dark place, figuratively and often literally. Life is precious because it is uncertain, and nowhere more so than in the tin mines, "a benevolent Moloch to whom [the miners] fed their children at an early age and from whom they took their daily bread."

The contrast to sunny Arizona could not have been greater, though Arizona, too, is a mining state. The capitol dome is clad in copper. The summer before my senior year in high school, my mom and I drove the two hours from Tucson to Bisbee, one of the largest copper mines in the world. The mine there is open pit—a term barely adequate to capture the stunning, gaping wound torn in the earth by machines the size of dinosaurs. It all seemed so mechanical, so "modern."

It was the contrast of the Bisbee mine that made us squirm so as we watched Ross Poldark and his men navigate the oppressive dark of the watery, twisting Cornish mines. There were no machines; mining was a battle of will and muscle against stubborn rock, fought in the dark, day after day, for years.

Graham's first novel captures the scene in the Poldark mine: "The walls here were streaming brown and green stained water, and in some places the roof was so low that they had to bend to get through. The air was foul and dank, and once or twice the candles flickered as if about to go out .... Soon the tunnel contracted until it became egg-shaped, about four-feet-six inches high and not above three feet across at the widest part .... The water came to just below the widest part of the egg, and here the walls were worn smooth with the rubbing of long-forgotten elbows."

My mom would shake her head. "You would never get me down there." She was the daughter of farmers, raised in the sun, the ground safely beneath her feet. "Would you go?" And though I secretly concurred, seventeen-year-old boys are not in the habit of agreeing with their mothers, or admitting to fear.

"Well, it would depend," I would say, like the lawyer I would some day become.

After all, Cornwall was very far away, and I assumed the old tin mines were closed. And, I thought naively, maybe the mines were just an atmospheric appendage, a sort of perverse hobby to supplement piracy and sheep. Gilbert and Sullivan never wrote operettas about tin mines, after all.

But I was wrong, as I learned all those decades after Poldark went dark. Like Cornwall itself, tin is very old. Before Christianity reached Cornwall, before Arthur and Merlin, before even the Romans, the men of Cornwall dug tin from the rocky soil and traded it by beast and ship to the corners of the known world.

It is a humble metal, a blue-collar metal, the hamburger helper of metallurgy. On its own, it seems flimsy–think tin cans, the tin man, or the tin soldiers I left scattered on the floor of my childhood bedroom. Where tin finds its courage is in combination with others. Mixed with antimony and lead it becomes pewter; painted on iron, it defies rust.

I have always loved ancient history. In the third grade, I gave my first—and so far only—lecture on the Trojan War to my mortified brother's sixth grade class. I had no understanding of the bronze swords that kept Ulysses and his men alive for twenty years. Cardboard copies were all my mother allowed in the house. Even less did I suspect or care about a link between Cornwall and Homer. How strange and wonderful,

then, to find my Cornwall journey mining memories, now seldom
recalled, from the shadows.

The Bronze Age itself was forged from the marriage of tin and copper.
Bronze is an alloy of tin and copper and sturdier than either parent alone.
And humble Cornwall is one of the few places in the world where copper
and tin are found side by side. The ancient Greeks wrote of tin from
Cornwall, and by the seventeenth century hundreds of tin mines, from
backyard pits to elaborate tunnels, ran beneath Cornwall. By the 1830s,
Cornwall produced two-thirds of the world's copper.

But men explore, and the world grows ever smaller. Even as the
Cornish mines strained ever deeper—tunneling beneath the ocean
itself—to find new riches, vast quantities of copper and tin were shipping
from Africa and Asia. The Cornish mines—and the toil of a hundred
generations—were abandoned. All that is left are the hundreds of empty
brick engine houses that dot the landscape like lonely chimneys, faded
sentinels of the empty honeycombs below.

The Geevor mine in Pendeen, ten miles south of St. Ives, was the
last mine to close. In 1990, busloads of Cornish miners marched in
London for their livelihood, but the government of Margaret Thatcher
refused further help. For all intents and purposes, four thousand years of
mining was history.

But Geevor remains open as a museum. Not as a quiet museum
behind glass, but as a working mine trapped in amber, as if it needed
only the miners themselves to spring back into action. Best of all, it is the
only tin mine in Cornwall where you can still follow in the footsteps of
the miners and go deep underground.

I thought of my mom. I thought of the two of us, all those years
before, hands paused over the popcorn bowl, shuddering at the thought
of squeezing through the tiny dark tunnels damp with the earth's sweat,
with only a single stubby candle to challenge the constant night.

Now, I had a chance to follow Ross Poldark into Cornwall's belly. I had a chance to say to my mom, watching I know from somewhere, "Look at me!" like a kid doing cartwheels in the sand. Do we ever stop wanting words of praise, of pride, even from the deceased?

All I needed was an opportunity and, if not courage, at least the benefit of forty years of rational thought. Tunnels don't just collapse, do they? Tourists don't just disappear into the depths, do they? I avoided all thought of piskies.

On an unseasonably sunny day, two of my fellow writers and I set out from St. Ives for Geevor. Before tackling the mine, we fortified ourselves at the Geevor cafe. In Cornwall, you are never far from tea or pasties. If I snuck a corner of my pasty into a napkin for later, it wasn't for the piskies. Absolutely not.

John and Kevin Hawkins sat at the table next to us. The brothers, both in their late forties, volunteer at Geevor, as do many former miners. John, the older brother, is an engineer who learned his craft on the job.

"Our grandfather worked at the mine when it opened, in 1911. Until the War. You can see his picture on the wall in the Mill," John said. He considered his family lucky. "No one died in the mine." The real danger, he said, was exposure to dust, and a miner in his thirties was considered old. "Mining paid well, considering. It was a way of life. And it was like a family. Look at the pictures."

Black and white photos of miners fill the corridors of the Mill where the miners clocked in, changed, showered, joked, cursed and prayed. Women were not welcome. They were considered bad luck underground.

It was a man's club, and a family club. Generations of men and boys worked side by side in the mines. Many of the tunnels were chipped and blasted only to the size of a youngster. It could take a day to flake away inches of rock, and the miners paid for tools, explosives, and even candles.

Pay was for tin ore only, by weight.

The women and girls worked above, but their jobs were no easier. Through the long summer and freezing winter days, the women and girls, called "bal maidens," crushed ore by hand. I imagined my mom complaining of sexism, but in truth I wasn't sure which job was worse.

In the cafe, we were joined by two young English couples on holiday. By now it was late afternoon, and the sun was headed toward the ocean just to the west of where we stood. We were in the last group to head underground.

Our guide gave us hard hats with headlamps and long raincoats, despite the blue sky. We soon knew why.

We paused in front of the tunnel entrance. It reminded me of a gold mine in an old western: two heavy vertical wood beams supporting a third, horizontal beam. It was dark inside. I half expected to see a rattlesnake, before getting a grip. Nothing to worry about, see, Mom?

I had to stoop to enter. Within ten feet we needed the headlamps to see. Another ten feet and the tunnel was ink black. I had forgotten what dark was until that moment. We in the modern world live with lights great and small: the neighbors, streetlights, passing cars, and even our host of digital companions. I gave silent thanks for the headlamps.

My companions and I walked and descended. The walls were rough and wet. The raincoats saved our clothes. We were careful with our hands—arsenic is in the rock. I stumbled more than once on the rough floor of the tunnel, and my back soon ached from stooping. We would squeeze through the narrow tunnel, one by one. To the sides were other intersecting, boarded-up tunnels.

The Geevor mine is actually a series of mines dating from Tudor times. From the surface, hundreds of tunnels and airshafts radiate out and down like the roots of a massive tree. One of the most remarkable museum exhibits is a three-dimensional model of the tunnel system, almost impossibly elaborate. Elevators were introduced only in the twentieth century; before that a man might climb up and down narrow wood ladders, an hour each way in the dark, to preserve candles.

Even with friends nearby, I had to suppress panic. The rough rock walls scraped my arms, and in places it was impossible to turn. At our feet we could see, in the gloom of the headlamps, tiny shafts that would have required a man to crawl—for how long?—on his belly. No, not for me—not with Mom, for Mom, or with the encouragement of a thousand piskies

We were finished within half an hour, though it seemed longer. The rock walls widened, and there I saw ... well ... the light at the end of the tunnel. I won't deny a sigh of relief.

I thought of the generations of men who preceded me in this tunnel, and far deeper. By the time Geevor closed, it was a "submarine" mine that extended out to and beneath the ocean. Our tourist tunnel was a faint taste indeed. But it was taste enough.

All those years ago I hedged. "It would depend," I had said. Well, the circumstances, the place, and the memories aligned in Cornwall. I guess it depended on an airplane, an opportunity, and a reason. Men like John and Kevin Hawkins preserve Geevor as a tribute to Cornwall's proud heritage, to the generations of Cornish families that worked the mines. As for me, the tribute may have been for just one, but here, where families gaze from photos and their footsteps echo, it seemed right.

And as I watched dusk descend, I was certain that here, in this place of ghosts, my mom was happy, too.

Cycling toward Penzance

# CYCLING CORNWALL

*Daphne Beyers*

"There's nothing out there," the young man warned me when I said I wanted to cycle to Land's End in Cornwall, England's westernmost point. I wanted to see the wind-swept cliffs jutting into the wild Atlantic; the crashing waves whose salt-spray could reach two hundred feet; the rugged, unspoiled moors, no good for farming or grazing—good for nothing, but good for me.

The young man meant well. For him Cornwall was a summer holiday, a place to surf and laze on sandy beaches. He didn't know that I was a connoisseur of nothingness; a gourmet of wild, empty places; a seeker of solitude. "Nothing" was exactly what I came to Cornwall to see.

As it turned out, "nothing" was pretty far away.

I was staying with friends in St. Ives, a resort town on the northern coast. Teeming with tourists, restaurants, pubs and shops, St. Ives was the opposite of nothing. I hired a bicycle, intent on escaping the crowded streets and heading into the wilds of Land's End. On the map, Cornwall seemed tiny. The entire United Kingdom can fit into California three times with room to spare. How far away could Land's End be?

I measured the distance on the map with my thumb, following the coastal road. The direct route as the crow flies would be only seven or eight miles, but winding all the way around the peninsula's coast, Land's End was eighteen miles from St. Ives, a thirty-six-mile round trip. I gritted my teeth. Thirty miles was as far as I'd ever cycled, and at the end of that journey, my legs were jelly. Six extra miles put Land's End as out of reach to me as the moon.

I could chance it. If I were in the Bay Area, maybe I would. Back home I had friends I could call if I ran out of steam, or I could call a cab, many of which are equipped with bicycle racks. I could even take a bus. But at Land's End there really was nothing: no cabs, no buses, no friends living close by. The same nothing I came to see would become my enemy. I had to find another route, one that cut out those six infinitely long miles.

After searching the map, my thumb measuring out miles like the gray fates measuring out mortal life, I decided Penzance was the key. Penzance was a town on the southern coast of Cornwall opposite to St. Ives, and a train connected the two towns. It was six miles to Penzance, the magic six miles I was looking for. I could cycle to Land's End then come back along the southern coast to Penzance and take the train the last six miles to St. Ives.

I had a plan, but it was already noon. For such a quest, I needed to get an early start. I decided to cycle the short distance to Penzance that afternoon and tackle Land's End another day.

I geared up—helmet, gloves, water bottle, and map—and headed out. My rental bike squeaked and groaned in places a bike shouldn't. Who knew how many people had ridden it before or how good the upkeep was? I shifted through the gears, and the squeaking quieted. The chain spun evenly with each pedal, not catching or stuttering on the teeth. The frame felt solid under my weight, the breaks caught when I pressed them, and the tires rode smoothly along the road, fatter than a road bike's and perfect for the rutty country lanes of Cornwall.

The wind buffeted my face as I soared downhill. I cut left and hit my first uphill. I downshifted and spun up the hill easily, only to be greeted by a second hill steeper than the first. Red brick houses lined the quiet neighborhood street. My thighs burned as I rounded another corner. The hill kept going up. I stopped and looked about me. I had no idea where I was. The street didn't have a name and wasn't on the map. I could see the beautiful sandy beaches of St. Ives far below, the crystal-blue water breaking white against the shore, the steeples of a church and the gable-roofed houses hugging the coast.

I hadn't left St. Ives yet, and I was already lost.

I found a workman and asked for the road to Penzance. Theoretically, he spoke English, the last native speaker of the Cornish language having died hundreds of years ago, but you could have fooled me. Fortunately, hand signs are universal, and from his gestures I gathered I'd gone too far uphill. I coasted back down the hill, wound through some lanes, and came to a roundabout with a sign pointing to Penzance. Not an auspicious beginning, but from there the road ran straight. An easy six-mile ride, I thought. What could go wrong?

I had been warned that Cornwall was hilly. I trained on hills at home. Even adjusting from feet to meters, the hills back home were higher and steeper than the ones in Cornwall. I should have been prepared, but in Cornwall, the hills were endless. On the road to Penzance, it was uphill, then down, then back up again, then down, then back up, again and again. It never ended. Every altitude I achieved was lost on the downhill and had to be regained through brute pedaling strength, all the way to Penzance. Worse still, my less-than-scientific measurements proved to be inaccurate. The ride to Penzance was nine miles, not six.

The scenery kept my spirits up. Once I passed the midway point, I could look down on rolling fields and pastures, all the way to the English Channel. St. Michael's Mount rose off the coast, a tidal island cut off from the mainland when the tide came in. A castle sat on the granite summit, the site of a former monastery. The island looked busy to me, that small bit of rock crammed with buildings and surrounded by fishing boats. It was the opposite of the nothing I'd come so far to see.

I coasted down to Penzance, called Pee-Zed by the natives. The town isn't considered a city, but it might as well be. Lorries hurtled down the traffic-jammed streets passing my bike by bare inches. I took to the sidewalk in self-defense where I soon became a hazard to crowds of pedestrians. A sign pointed to a national cycle trail. I veered off to follow it, leaving the crowds and belching traffic behind.

Traumatized by the noise and bustle of Penzance, I bolted two miles south to the quietude of Mousehole, a tiny hamlet of yellow-lichened houses huddled next to a fishing harbor. I stopped in the scenic town to consult my map. Not too far away, six miles in fact, stood the Merry Maidens, a circle of nineteen standing stones, remnants of Cornwall's prehistoric past. *Only six miles*, I thought. I was a little worried since I'd already pedaled further than I'd intended, but I wasn't ready to turn back yet.

On the mostly flat ride to Mousehole, I'd already forgotten Cornwall's hills, but the hills hadn't forgotten me. The only way out of Mousehole was straight up. In the lowest possible gear, my lungs blowing like a bellows, I climbed for two miles up and up and up. At the top, gasping for breath, I stopped at a T-intersection.

My legs shook with fatigue. I swigged from my water bottle and took inventory on my energy reserves. That last hill had exhausted me. The smart thing to do would be to turn right and head back to Penzance and home. Twelve miles of hills stood between me and St. Ives. I needed to tackle them before I ran out of strength. But I had made it to the Land's End peninsula, though not all the way to its end. That was too far a ride for that day, but I thought I could go a little further. I turned left.

Six-foot hedges lined the lonely country lane. It was barely wide enough for one car to pass. There was no shoulder to ride on if a car came, but I needn't have worried. There were no cars, no houses, no people, not even cows or sheep. For the first time I felt a glimmer of the nothing I'd pedaled so far to feel.

The way was smooth and flat for about a mile, long enough to convince myself I'd made the right choice. Then my tires began to pick up speed without me pedaling. I was going downhill. Downhill meant uphill soon after. I didn't think I could take another uphill. Cursing silently, I sped down the hill. There was nothing for it. I was already too far down to turn back.

The hill led to a narrow valley nestled among trees where the air itself turned emerald. Fallen leaves muffled the sound of my tires. It was a fairy glen straight out of Celtic myth. Golden glints of sunlight spun like silken threads through the air. A hushed silence permeated the place, broken only by the lazy gurgle of a brook. I was there and gone in an instant. My spinning wheels pulled me onward and upward, out of the glen. I didn't realize how magical it was until I left it behind and re-emerged into the ordinary world. I thought of going back, but these moments are gifts and cannot be taken by design. Going back could not recapture the moment. It had only been an instant, but in that instant I'd touched a magical eternity.

I pedaled uphill, a modest hill, a mere bump compared to the others, and then I was there, at the Merry Maidens and the end of that day's quest.

They say it's the journey not the destination, and so it was for me that day. The Merry Maidens were a letdown, at least for one seeking the absence of things. The stones stood in their cheerful circle, but tractor treads broke the ground through the center where some farmer took his shortcut. Whatever Druidic spell the sacred space once contained was long gone. They were just a bunch of stones now, an obstacle for tractors and irritated farmers, their once-sacred ring trampled by multitudes.

I made it back to St. Ives on sheer will. My easy jaunt had turned into a thirty-mile round trip. My legs were jelly. There was no way I'd make the thirty-six miles to Land's End and back on a second trip. If it were flat, maybe, but there were more hills to Land's End than to Penzance. The train wouldn't help either. The southern coastal route added more miles than the train subtracted. I knew I'd reached my absolute physical limit, Land's End hopelessly out of my reach.

Exhausted, I lay in bed that night and remembered the magical glen, the transporting instant of it, a sheer, fleeting moment that would be with me forever. I could never have planned that. This was Cornwall. I'd ridden its granite hills, imperturbable and unyielding. It wasn't going to change for me. I had to change for it.

I gave up my planning, gave up counting the miles with my thumb, and left my map behind. After a day of rest I rode out again, taking the way to Land's End though I knew I'd never get there. I'm still riding there as I write this, heading into the unknown, where the land gives way to the formless, the unplanned, where maps and compasses are useless, where even Cornwall's granite hills give way. Out of that formless ocean, unplanned and unexpected, miraculous moments happen in an instant and last for eternity.

Candles in the darkness

# MOORSTONES

*Anne Sigmon*

*A weight of awe, not easy to be borne,*
*Fell suddenly upon my spirit*

—From "The Monument" by William Wordsworth

At nearly one in the morning, the night was black around me—not even a sliver of moon to hang onto. Standing on the damp, foggy grounds of my English manor house hotel, I felt adrift, like an uneasy ghost wandering the moor. I struggled to make sense of the series of calamities that, over the previous six months, had battered—were still battering—the people I loved. My mother was dead. My brother-in-law's health was fragile. A miscarriage had cost my family a much-wanted child. One good friend's husband had died, another's was desperately, irretrievably ill. Two friends had lost sisters, far too young, to senseless tragedies. Now my cousin—only fifty-eight years old—faced what we all knew would be her final battle with cancer.

I felt cursed, like the precinct of my heart had been strafed by God.

My faith in shreds, my confidence in life shaken, I had come to Cornwall—English land of myth and ancient mystery—to rest my soul and to ponder the haunting fields of primal stone that had been sacred here for six thousand years.

I wondered what these ancient rock temples had meant to the stone- and bronze-age people who built them, and to the people who held them holy still. Could these enchanted stones speak to my unmoored heart? If so, what would they say?

The high granite plateaus of Cornwall—rocky outcrops, boggy moors, and windswept cliffs—harbor the greatest concentration of prehistoric stone monuments in Britain: colossal aboveground tombs known as *quoits* or *dolmen*; man-tall stone sentinels called *menhirs*, and enigmatic stone circles with magnetic properties and mysterious force fields. Many of these cryptic stones are aligned with each other, or with the sunset or sunrise on the equinoxes or solstices. It's a magical vista that has been invested with supernatural power since hunter-gatherer clans first settled here six thousand years ago.

The day before my midnight wanderings, I'd driven into Cornwall alone, heading south down Highway A30. As I crested a hill, the eighty-square-mile plain of Bodmin Moor stretched below me. Under circles of darkening clouds, the moor was a patchwork of yellowy bogs and shamrock-green fields. Crop and pastureland were cordoned into off-kilter rectangular and trapezoidal plots by hedges of dark granite called *moorstone*. The heft of these ancient walls was camouflaged by cascades of brushy plants. Towering above the landscape, imposing bald granite outcrops called *tors* jutted from hillsides. Like knots on a spiny massif, the *tors*—Rough Tor, Stowe's Pound, Tregarrick, Carn Brea, Trencom—slice through the center of the Cornish peninsula, coursing south toward the Celtic Sea.

Looking down from a highway viewpoint at this eerie landscape, I felt the weight of these primeval stones on my heart—the eons of life, hope, and death that have played out here. I shivered and skipped a breath, disturbed by a palpable force of time and inevitability.

Not far from my lookout, Tregarrick Tor stands on a small tributary of the River Fowey. It is, at a thousand feet, one of the highest points on Bodmin Moor. Some of Cornwell's earliest hunting bands once took refuge here. I imagined them clothed in bearskin hides, brandishing spear throwers, skulking through the undergrowth of a hazelwood and beech forest; Cornwall was covered by woodlands then. Life was short—about thirty years—and hard. Set on high ground, often near water, the *tors* offered shelter, warmth, and viewpoints to spot prey. Over time, wandering clans camped together at these points of sanctuary, to share information, seek mates and exchange gifts.

Perhaps these prehistoric hunters saw the *tors* as ancient buildings constructed by ancestor/creator gods. Maybe this is where clans from the north moved in and began to share astonishing information on how to take seeds from the plants they'd gathered and bury them in rows. People learned to water and fertilize the seeds and to coax emmer wheat, barley, lentils and flax from the rocky soil. They worked the ground with hand axe tools struck from hard volcanic greenstone found nearby, and fashioned flint sickles to harvest the grain. This was the dawn of a new age—the Neolithic, or new Stone Age—which lasted in Cornwall for fifteen hundred years, from roughly 4000 to 2500 BCE.

Incredibly, one of the first things these people did—just as they abandoned their hide teepees and settled into hamlets of thatched huts, before they built walls around the *tors* to enclose crop and pasture land—was to turn their eyes heavenward and build some of the most astounding structures known to history: megalithic stone tombs.

Called *quoits* in Cornwall (and, elsewhere, *dolmen*—which means "stone table"), these monuments became, over time, much more than gravesites. Visible from afar, the enormous structures marked clan territory. They also served as the focal point for community rituals and, historians believe, an emerging—and fervent—religion based on ancestor worship.

In the West, we no longer worship ancestors. Or do we? I thought of my father, dead for fifteen years. In life I'd always adored him. My promise to him to take care of my mother was the most solemn pledge I'd ever made. Now she had joined him. Their staunch Protestant faith had assured them—without question—that, after death, they'd be together in a tangible, sentient heaven. My own faith was murkier, of less comfort in loss.

Leaving my highway overlook, I drove toward Trethevy Quoit, one of the best-preserved megalithic tombs in Britain. Less than two miles away, it perches atop an ancient mound in an open field near the nineteenth-century Cornish mining village of Tremark Coombe. Known locally as the *Giant's House*, Trethevy is an immense stone rectangle with a slanting top, built about 3700 BCE.

I arrived in late afternoon. Skylarks twittered from trees at the edge of the field; the air smelled of grass and dried mud. The weather had cleared and filmy cirrus clouds drifted above the *quoit*. Its dark granite glittered golden in the sun.

The walls of the "house" are formed by six (originally seven) colossal granite slabs. They are, on average, ten feet tall—almost twice the height of the Neolithic men who raised them. The "roof" is a single twelve-foot capstone weighing well more than 20,000 pounds. Today it tilts wildly at about a forty-five degree angle, but once sat flat atop the walls. Most peculiar is a circular hole in the highest corner of the capstone that many antiquaries believe was used for astronomical sightings to mark the seasons. The chamber inside is large enough, archeologists say, to hold perhaps thirty bodies—clan leaders—who were buried with the weapons and treasures they'd need in an afterlife that they, like my parents, were sure would come.

After circling the monument for a time, awed by this crowning achievement of stone-age construction, I walked up the mound and stood in the shadow of the capstone. Shoving hard against a bulwark, I was struck by its immutable heft—a symbol of power and also, it seemed to me, of hope.

Trethevy Quoit and more than forty similar *dolmen* were raised in England in what archeologists describe as a seventy-five-year frenzy of building between about 3700 and 3650 BCE. This was a time long before wheels, pulleys or pack animals—and 1200 years before the miracle of Stonehenge or the earliest Egyptian pyramid at Sakkara.

I tried to imagine the effort of a hundred men—surely it would have taken that many, or more—laboriously striking greenstone into primitive choppers, fastening the stones with twine to wooden shafts. Straining, in burning sun and biting cold, they swung their axes and toppled trees, then stripped the branches to build rolling logs and dredges. Using all the might the community could muster, grunting and swearing men wrenched each stone onto the log sled, fastened it with leather straps, hauled the wobbly contraption over uneven ground, heaved the stones up an earthen ramp, and, with what seems to me inconceivable effort, hoisted the behemoths into place. It must have taken years.

Why? Why build this gargantuan granite temple instead of walls and hedges to protect their crops and pasture their animals, instead of boats to increase the yield of fish?

The answer, I thought, must lie in belief.

Archeologists say sites like Trethevy show that our stone-age ancestors believed in a journey to an afterlife. This was nothing new. Scholars now believe humans began to conceive of religion—god, spirit, salvation, afterlife—almost as soon as they could think. What some experts consider the world's earliest religious monument—celebrating ritual worship of the python—was erected in Botswana 70,000 years ago.

It's no different for humans today, I thought. The death of my mother and the suffering of my friends this year had provoked me to ask some hard questions about my own beliefs. What does it mean to cease to exist? What will it be like, when my time comes, to feel myself slip over the final precipice, into a black anesthesia of nothing? I've closed my eyes and tried, many times, to imagine it, but I can't. I can imagine myself lost, hurt, afraid, falling into protracted sleep. But even in extremis, I can't imagine myself without some hope of awakening.

Perhaps people have always felt this way. Over the millennia, they have conceived of a savior god-spirit in so many different ways. And, often, they've turned to stone as a durable symbol of shelter and hope for salvation.

Standing on the mound at Trethevy with my hand on the warm granite tomb, I felt the power in that space—the gravitas of great age and supreme effort—but also an aura of peace. It was as though, by being there, I was absorbing the faith the builders had in the ability of these god-blessed stones to save them.

It would be another three thousand years before descendants of these stone-age English forbears once again attempted to raise stone to godly heights. In the Middle Ages, about 1100 CE, they began to construct the great gothic cathedrals. Closest of these to Cornwall is the Cathedral Church of Saint Peter in Exeter, fifty miles from Trethevy Quoit.

On the afternoon I visited Exeter, twelve bells pealed the closing of the day from the 130-foot-high Norman tower. In the Lady Chapel, I bowed my head for evensong. Above me, pairs of trumpeting angels carved in medieval times paid homage to the Madonna shining down from fifteenth-century stained glass. As the voices of twelve *a cappella* choristers filled the vault of this great space, I imagined the heaven its builders saw.

As I left the service, an adjacent chapel door stood open. On the altar, in place of icons, a slat box heaped with river stones drew me in. Next to it sat boxes of pebbles, seashells, tiny pinecones, and wispy feathers. On the floor, votive candles flickered on a slab of slate, illuminating cairns that unknown supplicants had fashioned from the materials in these boxes. Tiny stone miniatures of the way-posts found by ancient graves, these cairns, I thought, must point the way toward the sacred, to the faith in the future that had abandoned me.

A tear trickled down my cheek as I bent over the boxes and chose a pretty mauve river stone—my mother's favorite color—a gray pebble, and a tiny feather, then arranged them on the stone altar with the others. One after another, I remembered loved ones who were in pain: my sister who, like me, grieved for our mother and worried about her husband; my cousin and my friends who faced incalculable loss. I closed my eyes and conjured their faces in happier times, wrapped each face in love and healing wishes, and, for each one, built a cairn, lit a candle, said prayers for deliverance, for healing, for faith, peace—and for hope.

Now we humans have come full circle, I thought, like the ancients, inclining to earth stones to help us face an uncertain future. I turned to leave the chapel, but some ineffable force held me back. I stood in the flickering candlelight feeling close to the spirits of those I loved. Finally I reached back into the boxes and pulled out stones, shells and feathers to build another cairn. This one was for me.

*And as I touch this stone*
*I feel the hands of those*
*My brothers*

*Who at dawn of human life*
*Erected to that same Old Sun*
*This temple of eternal praise, and thanked the*
*Source of Light and Love for just*
*Another day—to be alive.*

—From "The Stillness of This Hill"
by Edward Williams (1747-1826)

36

Lanyon Quoit

# CARN GALVA

*Tony Farrell*

Men-an-tol, Nine Maidens, Men Scryfa
scatter to the south
across moor to Lanyon.

Stones of the long dead.

And Carn Galva
—Stone Beacon—
the magnet that draws and pulls.

Above,
the sky pulses;
the freedom of flight
a distant roar.

And from the Galva
the sky is stitched
and trailed

with tracks
those travellers
cannot see.

Sky prints
that mark their passing.

Our journeys
a vapour trail
over the changing landscapes
of our lives.

Barbara Hepworth's *The Infant*

# BARBARA HEPWORTH:
# IN THE WARMTH OF HER FIRE

*Unity Barry*

*"If I didn't have to cook, wash up, nurse children*
*ad infinitum I should carve, carve, carve."*
—Barbara Hepworth

Her words jumped out at me from the wall of the Tate Gallery in St. Ives. Any woman with children can empathize with this mother, even if she isn't a towering genius of twentieth-century sculpture like Barbara Hepworth. I certainly empathized with the thirty-year-old artist who wrote those words. When the same age as Barbara I, too, had to balance work with motherhood. In my case though, I was single with only one child instead of four. Like her, I also had a fine arts education. The plan devised by my parents and high school counselors had been for me to teach after graduating from the San Francisco Art Institute. At the time it seemed like a logical way of working in my field of printmaking while supporting myself. By the time I graduated, the teaching jobs predicted to be plentiful had evaporated, and I gave in to the lure of a steady paycheck from big business.

Unlike Barbara, however, I didn't fully understand that the ethereal spark of creativity needs constant nourishment and use. Otherwise the fire dies. While mothering my daughter and working for a corporate employer I had allowed the flame inside me to grow cold. When I look at all Barbara endured, I wish I had a hundredth of her tenacious will, that I had not let life get in the way of my vision.

I had come to the Tate because a friend had advised that the Tate show of St. Ives artists, titled *International Exchanges, Modern Art and St. Ives 1915–1965,* merited a visit. With such a humdrum title I went with limited expectations, but I was certainly surprised. Along with Barbara's work, the exhibition included some of the twentieth century's most noted artists: Henry Moore, Piet Modigliani, Sam Francis, David Hockney, Alberto Giacometti, Constantin Brancusi, Wassily Kandinsky and Mark Rothko to name a few. I walked from piece to piece, exclaiming, "Look at this!" or "I didn't know *he* lived here!" I should not have been surprised. From the late Victorian period onward when construction of a railway to the area brought artists in droves to the formerly impoverished fishing village, the beauty and light of the area created an environment that still inspires artists. Although most represented at the Tate didn't actually live in St. Ives, during the last forty years of her life, Barbara did. These artists invited their friends to visit, and they in turn brought their muses. Inspiration blossomed in Cornwall, turning the remote area into a creative paradise.

That quote on the Tate Gallery wall accompanied a drawing Barbara had created during World War II. Jocelyn Barbara Hepworth was born on January 10, 1903, in West Riding, Yorkshire. She studied at the Leeds College of Art and the Royal College of Art, London. After traveling to Florence her sculpture placed second in the prestigious Prix de Rome, first place going to John Skeaping whom she married in 1925. Although she and Skeaping had one son, their marriage deteriorated until they divorced in 1933. She met painter Ben Nicholson in 1931, and they quickly became closely involved in their lives and work. Their triplets were born in 1934, but she and Nichols weren't able to wed until 1938, when his first wife finally agreed to a divorce. Hepworth and Nicholson became the central figures in London of the pre-war British avant-garde art movement.

In 1939 she and her family fled from London to Cornwall just in time to avoid the Nazi blitzkrieg. Cramped by impossibly small housing and wartime deprivations, she struggled to feed her family and care for the triplets, yet still found time and heart to create something momentous. After putting her children to bed every night she sketched, as she called them, her "sculptures in two dimensional form" into the wee hours of the morning. What might, to some, seem like insane overwork eventually paid huge dividends. She later rose to international fame as a pioneer in the post-war rise of abstract expressionism and gained a knighthood in recognition of her contribution to British art. Her work occupies major museums and public spaces throughout the British Isles, Europe, the United States, and around the world from Japan to Western Australia.

"A woman artist," she later maintained, "is not deprived by cooking and having children, nor by nursing children with measles (even in triplicate)—one is in fact nourished by this rich life, provided one always does some work each day; even a single half hour, so that the images grow in one's mind."

My story was so different from Barbara's. My daughter had grown and left home before I poked at the ashes of my creativity and rekindled the flame. Instead of returning to the visual arts: sketching, painting and lithography, my muse channeled my inspiration into creative writing— writing about the talents of great women artists whom I admired. In the years before visiting Cornwall, I finished my first historical novel, the story of Berthe Morisot. Berthe, a painter of soaring talent, was the female founder—along with the men now so famous—of Impressionism. Morisot successfully blended career with motherhood, an unheard of feat for a nineteenth-century French *grande bourgeoise*. Understandably, the struggles that talented women artists face loomed large in my preoccupations, and Barbara's life and work drew me inescapably to the warmth of her fire.

That fire was most evident at Trewyn. Also operated by the Tate, her nearby home, studio and sculpture garden display more of her true genius. From the cobblestoned street, the place is easy to miss with its small doorway and high wall surrounding the garden. Most of the smaller pieces occupy the inside spaces of what was once Barbara's home. One of my favorite examples of her work greets visitors at the top of the stairs to the main interior exhibition area. Carved from sable-hued Burmese wood in the year of her first son's birth, *The Infant* stands only a little over seventeen inches tall. In it Barbara uses the rounded forms that she later developed in her abstract expressionist work. The gesture of a baby's partially raised arms and pouting face captures a split second recognizable to any woman with children—the unspoken command, "Pick me up *now* or I'll scream!"

Walking around the room I worked hard to control my hands. I wanted to touch each piece, to caress the soft skin of a baby's bottom or stroke the interior curvilinear tube of a calla lily. Nor did it take much imagination to compare her rounded forms with the undulating landscapes of her native Yorkshire and adopted Cornwall. Later, I looked up some filmed interviews with Barbara and smiled in recognition. In them she firmly stated that only by touching sculptures could they be fully appreciated. Yes, Dame Barbara, I agree.

Outside in her garden, it seemed I had walked into a small corner of Eden. A tranquil space full of birdsong, it felt as if the outside world were miles away, not just beyond a wall screened by mature foliage and trees. She had designed the layout and selected the plants herself, specifically with her sculptures in mind. Each piece occupies a place chosen for the sightlines created and the light and shadow embracing it. Her sculpture bursts into life under the magical effects of sun and darkness. Light reveals and hides. Light dances and strokes. The signature holes that pierce her sculptures and reiterate the sensuous roundness of their forms also open up vistas beyond, like picture frames on a wall that separate art from its surroundings. Barbara turned her art into the frame and nature into the art.

One bronze, titled *Four Square (Walk Through)*, stands fourteen feet tall. Constructed from five almost square bronze slabs, four pierced by large circles, Barbara created this with a sense of urgency after receiving a cancer diagnosis. The slabs form a structure that feels architectural and when a Tate Gallery attendant encouraged me to walk through it, I jumped at the chance. In fact, the Tate honors Barbara's desire to share the sensuality of her work by permitting visitors to touch the pieces in the garden. After all, whatever can hold up to the Cornish elements can certainly hold up to caressing by human hands.

I chatted with the gallery attendant about the obviously strong relationships between Henry Moore's work and Barbara's. The two artists were good friends from their twenties, when they met in art school, until her death in 1975. The attendant mentioned a fact that is neither posted anywhere in the museum nor written about in the books I purchased from the gallery bookstore. I found the small fact massively important: Both sculptors are famous for the revolutionary technique of piercing their work. Moore's international standing as a genius rests partly on those hollow spaces. Yet, the first time Barbara completed a piece with a piercing, Moore visited her studio the next day. *His* first piece with an aperture appeared only after seeing hers. I couldn't help thinking about Berthe Morisot and how she pioneered some of the Impressionist painting techniques earlier and pushed them further than famous men such as Renoir and Monet. Like Barbara, she too still lives in the shadow cast by men.

It occurred to me that women like Barbara Hepworth and Berthe Morisot were *my* muses. True I'd given up the brush, but I had returned to the world of art with the written word, and even though Barbara Hepworth seemed to have a much more tenacious will than I, I had my own tenacity and fresh determination to attain my own artistic goals: to bring these women artists of genius out from by the shadows and into the light of their due recognition.

Lynne Rutan, her instructor, and her tasty pasty

# IN PURSUIT OF THE PROPER PASTY

*Lynne Rutan*

Sweat beads under my bangs. Flour clings to my cheek, my plastic apron and my hiking boots. I am a culinary tourist in pursuit of the pleasures of my appetite, and once again, I am up to my elbows in the ingredients of a culture. This time, it's a Cornish pasty baking class in Falmouth, England. I'm here to learn to make the region's signature meat-and-vegetable turnover. This is not aerobics, so why am I working so hard?

It is to redeem myself. My teacher Charlie Choak and fellow students, Alistair and Mike, Cornishmen born and bred, laugh when I speak the name of the local dish I want to learn to make. "Pass-ti, it's pass-ti," Charlie enunciates, as if to a toddler. I laugh, too, embarrassed by my unintended slur. Unknowingly, I had pronounced "pasty" to rhyme with "tasty," equating the hallowed Cornish meat pie with the American stripper's most minimal cover.

What a mistake! In Cornwall, the crescent-shaped pasty has sustained the hearty miners, farmers and workers of this rugged country for centuries, perhaps even a millennium. The pasty has spawned about as many legends as the fabled King Arthur and his knights, who, the story goes, also indulged. The traditional Cornish pasty is so revered that St. Carantoc is its patron saint. The town of St. Morvah holds an annual

Pasty Day. The European Union has given it Protected Geographical Indication Status, which means by law a pasty can't be called Cornish unless it comes from Cornwall.

Fortunately, everyone seems amused rather than insulted by my pronunciation gaffe, and Charlie continues our lesson. His family's bakery, JH&M Choak, has been selling pasties since 1948, and Charlie teaches with the authority of fifty years in the business. Wiry and strong, his back has been bent and his sinewy arms sculpted by decades of pasty production, slinging loaded baking pans, and pursuing his other passion: sailing the Cornish coast. A Choak's Pasties baseball cap restrains hair as white as the flour that covers his black apron.

Our classroom is the unpretentious bakery itself. Its sky-blue storefront on Killigrew Street faces a quiet square just off Falmouth's main thoroughfare. In one big room, a couple of metal work tables and several commercial ovens share space with a simple retail counter and display cases. Through big picture windows we can watch the street scene, while passersby look in on our progress.

Charlie has already prepared the pasties' innards: a mix of thinly sliced squares of raw potato, onion and yellow-orange swede.

"What's a swede?" My question creates some tension between Charlie's English English and my American English, but my classmates pitch in with their ideas and we reach détente, concluding that a swede translates to rutabaga or yellow turnip in the U.S.

In a separate bowl, Charlie has sliced and diced skirt steak. While the best kinds of vegetables and their proportions can be debated, the law requires that an official Cornish pasty must contain at least 12.5 percent meat. Charlie shrugs at such hairsplitting. He allows as how purists would not object to flank or chuck for flavor and also because they produce enough juice to create a gravy. He seasons everything with salt and white pepper—"not black" he emphasizes and warns us, "Err on the side using too little." I'll recall his advice when my own first attempt tastes like it has been dunked in seawater.

To prepare the dough that will encase the meat and vegetables, Charlie cuts margarine and pieces of lard into flour until it looks like pebbles and sand. Adding water very slowly he uses his fingers to mix the dough into a soft ball. The dough, Charlie explains, must cool and rest for twenty-four hours to improve its elasticity, so into the refrigerator it goes. We'll work with a well-rested batch he'd made the day before.

"What about using butter instead of margarine and lard?" I ask.

Charlie bristles and snaps, "No, much too rich, only lard and margarine will do."

I won't argue with my teacher—imagine the humiliation of flunking Pasties 101—but secretly I vow to experiment back home.

Pasty pastry, unlike the wimpy stuff of so many baked goods, is as tough as the country women who perfected it. "You can work it and mix it as much as you want," Charlie claims. As his fingers massage the dough, he shares some of the facts and folklore that surround the dish that has nourished Cornish history.

For at least 3000 years Cornwall has been a land of tin and coal mines, clay pits, quarries and farms—all run on the sweat and blood of a hardworking labor class. The pasty—a cheap, well-balanced and hearty meal in its own carrying case—sustained families in the fields and miners during long hours in dark and dangerous tunnels. The miners worked deep underground with arsenic, without an opportunity to wash up before lunch. Charlie says the miners ate the pasty's filled center and discarded the thick crimped handle of dough to protect themselves from the poison on their hands. With a simple efficiency, the crusts were thrown to the rats, the miners were fed, and the vermin were dead.

I've since read contrary accounts, that the thrifty, hungry miners would never throw away a bite of food. Pictures show them eating pasties wrapped in muslin and paper. Others claim the miners threw the crusts to the "knockers," those heard-but-unseen spirits whom the superstitious miners believed could be malicious if not fed and appeased.

Ramping up his Cornish brogue with a twinkle in his eye, Charlie explains that some long-ago miner's wife lowered his meat pie down to him tied to a string, but in the black tunnel he couldn't find it. She kept letting out more and more string until, in exasperation, she yelled down "it's past ye" and the name stuck, even if the miner never ate that day.

My Cornish classmates hoot in disbelief at our teacher's version of the origin of the word. Emma Mansfield, in *The Little Book of The Pasty*—a delectable morsel of a book that bulges like a pasty with everything you ever need to know about the dish—contends plausibly that the name began with a thirteenth century French word "*pastee*" or "*pastez*," that morphed into early English as "paste," meaning "made of pastry."

My teacher is on the verge of losing his cred as a historian until Terry Audley, our all-knowing guide in St. Ives, tells a story similar to Charlie's, even giving the name of the mine where it happened and a name to the miner's wife—Mrs. Zacharias. Who knows for sure? What is true is that even though most of the mines have closed, pasties have become big business, contributing over $100 million a year to the economy. In towns like St. Ives and Falmouth, there is a pasty bakery on nearly every block.

Charlie may be a better storyteller than historian, but he is at his best—world class—as a pasty crimper. In less time than it takes to tell, he rolls out a perfect circle of dough; squeezes a palm-sized gob of the vegetables to get the liquid out; spreads it on the center of the disk; and lays a red line of meat across the middle. Before folding the dough over the meat and vegetables he moistens a side and pinches the edges together.

Then Charlie's fingers begin to flow across the rough seal in time to his mantra: "roll over, tuck and move." With his left thumb as a guide, he folds the dough over his right thumb and pushes in the flap with his right index finger. Each time his thumb slides, a perfectly rounded crimp appears in the stretchy cream-colored dough, then another, and another.

And now, it's my turn. I don't have too much trouble with the prep—well, to tell the truth, the lines of my dough circle wobble a bit, and my fingers turn to sausages, flaccid and unresponsive, when I try to crimp the seal. Despite Charlie's exhortations, my left thumb refuses to lie still to be covered by the pastry flap, and my right index finger can't catch it to make the tuck. I'm sweating and every muscle in my torso and arms has tightened with concentration and effort. By now Charlie has repeated his demonstration, "like this," so many times he is back to speaking to me like a toddler.

My classmates struggle too, but they don't have too many expectations. They are Charlie's boating buddies. "He roped us in last night at the pub," they freely admit. I wasn't at the pub; I'd seen the class advertised on the Internet and had signed up stone cold sober. I'd assumed that my previous cooking lessons in France and Belgium and a stint in professional culinary school would somehow equip me to sail through the class.

How could anything so simple create such anxiety? Generations of Cornish wives turned out these things in ill-equipped cottage kitchens nearly as dank and uncomfortable as the mines in which their men folk toiled.

How can beef stew in a purse be so difficult to reproduce?

Finally, Charlie's repetitions and demonstrations click in to connect my brain to my fingers and my swirling crimps begin to look full and more uniform. I egg-wash my best effort and send it to the convection oven, from which it emerges about a half hour later.

I'd forgotten that the pasty crust, even in the cold underground, kept the filling warm until miners had their "crib" or lunch. Charlie warns me to be careful, but I can't wait to take a bite, and my pasty burns my mouth. The crust is more tough than flaky—this novice crimper proved one CAN overwork the dough. I'd also over-salted the contents, and the crimp is a touch too dark.

Even so, *my* pasty, golden brown with a lovely crimped seam, is a thing of beauty to behold and taste—at least in my eyes and mouth. The meat is tender, the vegetable chunks cooked just past crisp, and the flavors have run together in a full-bodied sauce.

I'm pleased, but more important, my teacher approves, handing me a fully laminated Certificate of Training to prove I've been "successful in making a Proper Cornish Traditional Pasty." In the Land of King Arthur and his Knights of the Roundtable, I am now certified to search for the holy grail of pasties, that proper pasty that sets the mouth of every true Cornish man and woman to watering.

Obsessed, I wander around Cornwall from pasty shop to pasty shop, tasting and comparing. In St. Ives, a tourist town world famous for its sand beaches, scenery, quaint architecture and art, I only have eyes for bakery windows that feature the golden D-shaped treats. Over the course of three hours, one day, sampling the wares of five shops, I soon feel like an overstuffed Goldilocks. Some pasties are too salty, some unseasoned. Some are too tough, some crack with a bite. Some have too little meat, some too much.

But where's the one that's just right?

"I wouldn't buy one from a shop," our guide, Terry, says when I enlist him in my quest. "Who's to know what's in it."

The clannish Cornish people and the whole pasty baking industry might find Terry's opinion suspect—he hails from Dorset, after all, and has only lived in Cornwall for forty-four years—but for him "there's nothing like a proper homemade pasty." Every Thursday he is in town, Terry dines on "piping hot" pasties prepared by Mary Vinniconve, a friend's mother. "She got her recipe from her mom, who got it while living in a mining town," Terry says. "My mate claims his granny used to crimp with her false teeth."

Terry praises the quality of the minced beef she uses and the white turnips because "they're less likely to go mushy than swedes." But most important, Terry extols the care his friend's mother takes in her preparation. It's a full day operation worth every minute of work when her pasties bring her family home each week.

I've gotten my hands—and my mouth—around the pasty, its taste, its crimp and its meaning to the Cornish people. After talking with Terry—and suffering indigestion from my marathon taste testing—it's time to give up my quest for the perfect pasty until Mrs. Vinniconve invites me to dinner. Meanwhile, I plan to investigate some other local specialties.

Anyone for some Cornish clotted cream—and then, perhaps, a stint at Weight Watchers?

Sir Galahad

# Had It with Galahad

*MJ Pramik*

If I couldn't find my Sir Galahad in the land of King Arthur, where could I find him? In search of the Holy Grail of "relationship," I'd travelled to Cornwall—a thin peninsula of England jutting west into the Atlantic and, literally, home to many a romantic tale.

After a sad divorce, a psychic hurt, and supporting three children through college, I was still fiercely resisting any resemblance to *Business Girls*, English poet laureate Sir John Betjeman's poem about a certain destiny. Betjeman is buried at St. Enodoc's Church in Trebetherick, Cornwall. Lines from *Business Girls* seemed to aptly summarize my current state of affairs:

> And behind their frail partitions
> Business women lie and soak ...
>
> Rest you there, poor unbelov'd ones,
> Lap your loneliness in heat.
> All too soon the tiny breakfast,
> Trolley-bus and windy street!

I'd waited a respectful twelve years after the divorce before venturing forth on a soulmate search. I was ready. It was time. I warmed up for my quest by trying a few online dating services.

OkCupid turned out to be OkStupid, a "free" online source. Yes, you get what you pay for. Their algorithm matched me with a nineteen year old and a thirty-one year old, the former younger than my son and the latter, the age of my eldest child.

The next service, eHarmony, also proved unsuccessful. Their algorithm for matching people appeared to highlight age. I'm at a disadvantage with this statistic because, chronologically, I'm old(er). I use "35 years" on the YMCA exercise machines to gain a modicum of traction on the elliptical apparatus, while an online mental quiz has me pegged at "31 years." My friends rate me a passable "47 years" when I'm wearing makeup. Family genetics contribute—Dad remained virile and interested in women into his nineties, and Mom, through sheer orneriness, outlasted her siblings by at least twenty years. Life is not chronological, of course, but to many men it is. I live in all dimensions at once, still my fifty-eight-year-old eHarmony match freaked at the "actual age" number on my profile.

"eHarmony must have made a mistake!" he insisted. "I usually date women in their forties."

Oh.

Once in England, I admired London friend Filiz's practicality and luck. She'd made a successful match via *The London Times* personals. Visiting Feliz in her lovely home in Kingston upon Thames, I listened to her lectures on my continuing research. Serious and focused, she presented me with a book she thought might help—*The 60-Day Man Plan: How to Find and Keep the Man of Your Choice* by Margaret Kent. An American attorney, Kent outlines how to interview and find a partner. I read the entire book on the five-hour train journey to St. Ives.

Following Kent's instructions, I filled a collection of index cards with questions, hoping this would translate into finding a beau.

Day Eight into *The 60-Day Man Plan* challenge, I visited Tintagel, legendary site of Arthur's court situated on the north Cornish coast. The "castle"—a collection of ruins, reconstructed walls and magnificent wooden staircases—delights Arthurian Round Table seekers. Descending draconian step cascades toward the main constructions, I passed a very elderly gentleman. Resplendent in white beard, pale complexion, and beige wide-brimmed hiking hat, he whispered, "He was our greatest king."

"Yes, indeed he was," I replied. This man channeled Merlin's phantasm. A reverence affected the remainder of my Tintagel wanderings.

An ageless spirit surrounds the site. The "chapel"—a designated area of layered stones ranging from a foot high to several feet forming a rectangle atop one knoll at the site—revealed a man of medium age, a shaved head, a "Brooklyn" T-shirt, and interesting vibes. We descended together from the chapel.

"Please go ahead," I suggested. "I step slowly on these stairs." I nodded toward the steep-angled slate slabs, my knee brace hidden under tan hiking pants.

"I would like to. Should you slip, I'll catch you." This flirtation fit right into *The 60-Day Man Plan*—chivalrous, most important. His British accent triggered a heart flutter.

"You're not from Brooklyn?" I observed.

"Someone gifted me with this shirt," he replied, his gray eyes holding me in their steady gaze.

We stepped out of the site and headed toward Merlin's cave. The cavern, walled with slate and volcanic rocks and about 330 feet in length at sea level, sits beneath the ruins of Tintagel Castle. Alfred Lord Tennyson holds that this is where Merlin ferried the infant Arthur for safekeeping, and this is where my not-from-Brooklyn gallant evaporated.

The next day, to improve my chances of meeting a knight not-quite-so-errant, I intended a pilgrimage to the medieval Madron Well that lies in a boggy area a quarter mile from the Madron village in the large rural parish of the same name north of Penzance.

Darkness fell as friends Anne and Daphne and I neared Madron. Reading road signs required squinting and strain and squeezing my pupils into sharp pinpoints of pain. In Madron, we stopped at the King William the Fourth Inn, where the establishment's six patrons carefully considered my question, "Where is the Madron Well?"

"I'm the best one to ask that of, my dear. Let me direct you." The graying gentleman escorted me out to where our car rumbled. "You continue down the road here to the right, past the cemetery. Watch for the signs tacked about on trees and posts. You're only ten minutes from the well. If you can't find it, I'm here tomorrow." He grinned, raised his hand to his silver tresses, and disappeared into the pub.

The gray cavalier's directions were spot on. Zipping past the cemetery, we directed iPhone flashlights toward all shapes resembling signs. "The Well," in faded red paint, appeared on one. We veered right and bumped down an unpaved country lane into a parking area.

To make use of every ounce of remaining twilight, I hopped out of the car and strode briskly down a tree-canopied lane. Anne and Daphne followed. Tripping along on the nearly invisible path, I felt pulled as if by a magnet to … the Cloutie tree.

Cloutie trees—prayer trees infused with the spirit of Gaia and ancient beliefs—rank high as Celtic pilgrimage sites. Protocol for cloutie trees requires that pilgrims affix bits of fabric to the limbs. Each cloth tie includes petitions for healing, spiritual growth and soul connection. At Madron, the tree is a blackthorn with branches reaching from bog to heaven.

Only vague shapes of branches and brambles surrounded the path.

I continued unafraid. After fifteen minutes of stumbling, the Madron Cloutie—resplendent in dangling ribbons, rainbows of fabric and torn paper shards—burst out of the blackness. I had arrived at my grail. Fumbling with my flashlight, I circled the tree. Selecting a slim branch over the central bog, I laced my ribbon and my request around the Cloutie's damp wooden finger.

Anne and Daphne joined me, adding their intentions. Time had stopped. Darkness protected us as if a warm cloak. We walked back quiet and subdued, wrapped in our own musings.

The morning after our ritual at the Madron Cloutie, I chose to hike the Coastal Trail. My day began in Zennor, where D.H. Lawrence—huddled in a small cottage writing *Women in Love*—spent several years with lover, Frieda Weekley. The morning rose, glorious. A Cornwall-blue horizon opened up over pastures and a one-lane country trail. Google Maps posted a one-hour-and-forty-three-minute time for this trek.

I traipsed past rural architecture and quiet farms. An exhilarating quiet hovered. Only a slight zephyr murmured as I crested the first ninety-plus-degree slope. Then reality struck: The terrain steepened critically as far as the eye could see. My idealized rolling coastal hike had just evolved into a mountain climbing expedition.

"Oh, gee (expletive deleted)!"

Stretched out before me as far as my eye could see was the "severe" Coastal Trail. This meant strong climbing to achieve the peak lying beyond the next crest. One path downward kissed the shoreline. Steep rocky descents of boulder cluttered an ambiguous trail and even steeper ascents up topped peaks.

Glancing at my watch, I hopped over and down a mud-wrapped trail. Then there occurred, quite literally, a turn of events: I watched the slow-motion skid of my left ankle on angled rock. My foot bent inward a full ninety degrees accompanied by a LOUD pop and crunch.

"Oh (more expletives deleted)!"

Hefting myself up by grasping at brambles, I discovered I could not put weight on the ankle. "Searing pain" describes it well. I turned down my sock. My ankle had swollen to a nauseating three times normal. I might need to use my medevac insurance. One small problem: No cell signal bounced out on the Cornish coast. I couldn't even call St. Ives Ace Taxi to retrieve me.

For the next two hours I acted out a scene from Daphne du Maurier's *Jamaica Inn* where protagonist Mary Yellen (aptly named) kidnapped by the vicious albino minister, Francis Davey, flees with him over the moor.

"They scrambled up the hill amongst the boulders and slabs of
granite, ... and they waded in and out of crevice and rock,
knee deep in soaking bracken and black heather, climbing ever
higher and higher to the great peak of Rough Tor. ... the granite
was monstrously shaped, tortured and twisted into the
semblance of a roof, and Mary lay beneath the great stone
slab, breathless, and bleeding from her scratches ..."

Yup, du Maurier must have crossed this exact spot on the Coastal Trail during one of her many Cornish outings. With swollen lower limb, I completed all of two trail miles in three hours.

As the day advanced, other hikers appeared. A young extreme athlete who'd run from the St. Ives direction said he'd covered four miles to my current location, meaning my return trip was a long one. Focused on his time, he checked his watch, inquired if I was all right, and then sped off without waiting for my reply. Next, a serious group of hikers passed: three men and a woman. The man carrying the map acknowledged my plight and suggested I find the next public footpath out to the road where I might hitch a ride to St. Ives.

Sitting on a monstrous boulder, engorged ankle pulsing with pain, I weighed my options. "Morose" might best describe my mindset.

"Hello, are you all right?" There before me, handsome and cheerful, stood the Galahad of my imaginings. Real name, David, from North London. The Madron Cloutie tree worked overnight! "Here, take my hiking pole," he offered. "I've got another in the car. I do have two good legs. The public path is at the signpost atop this hill."

Awestruck, I could only stammer mumbled thank you's.

"Here, let me adjust this pole for your height," he continued. "Are you sure you are all right?"

"Yes, yes." I always claim independence and feeling "all right" when I am not all right.

As I set off from the monstrous boulder, limping uphill, David made another suggestion. "Perhaps I should walk with you."

"Oh no, please, don't spoil your hike any further." Now why did I say that? Margaret Kent of *The 60-Day Man Plan* would have slapped my wrists for the gaff.

"Are you certain?" David had such clear honest eyes.

"Oh yes." Well, no, not really. "Thank you again for the pole."

Another opportunity missed. Flustered by his gallant gesture, I failed to ask his full name and address to return the pole!

The public path proved flatter, yet more than a mile from the road. Cool thickets of blackberries loomed on both sides. No bulls charged as I limped across their pastures. The hiking pole allowed me to pick up speed. On reaching the nearly two-lane road, I rechecked my mobile phone. Still no signal. Only a few cars and delivery vans passed. Finally, a middle-aged couple with two dogs and a van with a bed constructed inside it, stopped. On their way to Fowey, they changed course and drove me to St. Ives, Tregenna Castle … and ice.

In her book *Enchanted Love*, writer and spiritual teacher Marianne

Williamson explains the mystical power of loving relationships: "Our deepest human need is not material at all: Our deepest need is to be seen. We need adventure. We need meaning. We need identity. We need love. Someone who has seen us through loving eyes has awakened us from the ranks of the formerly dead."

I may not have found a Galahad for keeps, but David's kindness calms my heart. I placed a wish on the Cloutie tree and believe I've been seen.

Upon returning home, I posted a "Lost and Found" advertisement in *The London Times Saturday* and the *London Review of Books*.

Advert: DAVID - Leki Hiking Pole Gifted on St. Ives-Zennor Coastal Trail, Oct 3, Love to return pole. Mary    Email

No response to date. I keep checking.

The honeysuckle

# THE HONEYSUCKLE VINE

*Kitty Hughes*

When I asked a Cornishman what he knew about the honeysuckle vine, he drew a blank. "I know nothing about it," he replied, "except that my mother said, 'It's bad luck. Never bring it in the house.'"

"Why?" I persisted.

He shrugged his shoulders.

Why didn't his mother want it in the house? Was it the strong fragrance or its purportedly poisonous berries? Was her warning an allusion to some long-buried impropriety?

*Yes*, I thought, *that may be the reason.* The honeysuckle vine twists clockwise, wrapping through time, sensual, scented and infused with desire. Its tube-like blooms, in pale yellow or white, wind through my memories from the time of early innocent pleasures to the hot flower-festooned hideaways of my teenage years. Its fragrance infused the humid summer air as I was growing up in the southern state of Arkansas. As children, my friends and I pulled off the tips and drew down the sweet syrup between puckered lips. We threw big-eyed glances at each other, claiming that ours was the sweetest, and laughed.

On broiling evenings, when the temperature refused to drop, my father would pile us all in the family station wagon and tool around town to cool us off. My sisters and I enjoyed the summer air through the open windows as we lounged in the back seat. The cloying odor of honeysuckle, magnified by the heat, rode in on the breeze, and is forever linked in my mind with the taste of the ice cream cones at the Dairy Queen where we would always stop.

Shortly before my Cornwall trip, I had read the twelfth-century Breton lay by Marie de France, *Chevrefoil* or *The Lay of the Honeysuckle*, translated by Eugene Mason, which relates one of the oldest Cornish legends: the illicit love between the famed lovers Tristan and Iseult. In Marie de France's version of the story, Tristan compares his and Iseult's love to an intimate union in the plant kingdom, that of the honeysuckle that wraps around the hazel tree.

Before I boarded the plane for England this poetry wound itself into my brain. I thought to find honeysuckle growing rampantly, woven like a thread through the countryside as myths are woven into cultural memory.

If you don't remember the legend of Tristan and Iseult, Tristan is banished from England when King Mark discovers that his wife, Queen Iseult, and Tristan love each other and have been meeting privately. Marie de France's lay picks up the tale when Tristan returns from his exile in South Wales, desperate for Iseult's love.

Tristan learns from the peasants that the king has summoned all his barons to Tintagel, where he plans to hold court at Whitsuntide "with feasting and good sport." Knowing the route the queen will take to the castle, Tristan lies in wait for her in the forest. He places a private signal for her along the path, one that he has used before, and knows that when she sees it, she will stop and draw off into the woods to meet him.

All of this private signaling, surreptitious meetings, and love-talk outside the bounds of marriage are part and parcel of the conventions of medieval courtly love. Sensuality is magnified by abstention. The lover must maintain a public formality and distance, while breaching the walls of conventional love.

In the case of Tristan and Iseult, the attraction is especially forbidden, dangerous and lethal: She is a king's wife, he a mere knight. Presumably, all the more delicious. What actually happens in the woods with Iseult, we are never told. The rules of courtly love dictate secrecy and discretion, and the consequences of discovery are dire.

In Tristan's own language, he and Iseult cannot be pried apart, suggesting a sexual coupling, as well as a necessary symbiosis and a matter of life and death. He describes their love in an elaborate metaphor:

*For we are like the honeysuckle vine*
*Which around a hazel tree will twine,*
*Holding the trunk as in a fist*
*And climbing until its tendrils twist*
*Around the top and hold it fast*
*Together tree and vine will last.*
*But then, if anyone should pry*
*The vine away they both will die.*
*Dearest, we're like that vine and tree;*
*I'll die without you, you without me.*

Tristan does not mention the vine's fragrance, but he does refer to the leaf, called *"chevrefoil"* (goat leaf) in French. According to my gardener husband, it is so named because the leaves resemble a goat's hoof print and it is said goats like to eat it. The sexual implication of "goatiness" is hard to avoid.

If you have ever inhaled the honeysuckle's scent, you know the allure of its sensuous perfume. In William Faulkner's novel, *The Sound and the Fury*, the character of Caddy reacts with Pavlovian urgency when she gets a whiff of the vine. Whenever she mentions it, you know that sex is near, both as desire and fulfillment. Perhaps that Cornish mother knew what she was talking about.

I was particularly keen on finding honeysuckle vining near the craggy remains of Tintagel Castle, perhaps on the very path where Tristan waylaid Iseult for their private tryst. There is indeed a single path that descends to the castle from the center of town, rimmed with thick hedges of hawthorn enmeshed with a proliferation of climbing vines. I scanned the hedges in vain, as I wended my way down toward one of the most spectacular views in Cornwall.

The closed-in path rises to a broad lookout over the castle ruins perched on high rocks over the Atlantic's blue expanse. Wind, rain and ocean spray have eroded the walls of what may have been King Arthur's Court, now crumbled suggestions of chambers and archways. A stone staircase descends and narrows before twisting back up to the ruins, weathered stacks of ragged stone.

I did not find honeysuckle, but I did dream the division of the two spheres—the private and the public: the sheltered path, where trysts and skirmishes and other shillyshallying could occur, and the exposed life of the court, with its formal spaces and rituals.

I was disappointed, of course, not to find my prize, but I kept looking. I sought out honeysuckle everywhere in Cornwall: in the fenced-in cottage plots, the rambling estate gardens, and the sprawling woods around the Tregenna Castle Hotel in St. Ives where we were staying. It refused to appear on the sloping paths of the Heligan Gardens, in or near the giant Biomes of Eden Project, or along the cliffs by Geevor Mine at St. Just, where weeds scramble over rocks brought up from the tunnels below.

I asked gardeners about the honeysuckle, as well as florists. I asked for honeysuckle jam at the grocer's. I asked the woman selling potted herbs at the farmers' market at the St. Ives Guild Hall if she grew honeysuckle. Mindful of its clockwise twist, I saw such a vine spiraled firmly up a wooden pole in the Barbara Hepworth Museum and Sculpture
Garden; but it turned out to be jasmine. No one seemed to know much about the honeysuckle, real or represented, or where to find it.

"You just won't find it in here, in any way, shape or form," one of my travel companions remarked, having checked her botanical guide to Cornwall and found no mention of it. I texted my husband who assured me, "Of course it is there. It grows all over Europe."

Several residents reminded me that it was too late in the year for it to be in bloom, although it volunteered in their gardens in the summer. I didn't meet anyone who associated honeysuckle with poetry or myth, or in any way with Arthurian legend.

I was beginning to think I was on a fool's errand. The summer foliage was indeed fading, and my gardener husband warned, "You may have come too late."

On the last full day of my trip, I took the bus from St. Ives to Penzance to visit the Trewidden Garden. There it finally showed up. A full mop of it was draped over the Welcome Center near the front gate. It was almost a little joke—a humble, unkempt vine allowed to adhere to the wall at the entrance of a rather pretentious estate and its formal gardens with espaliered apple and pear trees and manicured, carefully placed varieties of palms, ferns and hydrangeas.

The flowers were in perfect bloom and exuded a lingering scent. I picked one, a delicate yellow, with thin petals and stamens protruding from the middle, dusted with a dab of pollen. I took a couple of long inhales and I was transported back to another place and time. Quests can lead you back to yourself, and I suppose that is what happened to me.

In my teens, there were some illicit pleasures. On summer nights my boyfriend would tap on my bedroom window with a blanket in hand. We escaped into the woods in a still undeveloped area that lay behind my house. There, surrounded by honeysuckle vines that looped around white oak trees, we threw ourselves down on the blanket and proceeded to engage in some serious making out. We went at it for hours, mindfully aware that we had to sneak back before midnight and make it to school the next morning.

Like the medieval lovers, we had our rules: no undressing or going all the way. We rubbed against each other with all our clothing on, releasing adolescent hormones again and again, in the steamy scented air. I didn't permit, or barely permitted, any exploration of my breasts, even through the cloth. I would fend off those attempts with a swift repositioning of my boyfriend's hands.

All summer long, the scent of honeysuckle hung in the sultry air, rich and heavy. I am older now, and the scent lingers in memory, reminding me especially of a time when the smell of that weedy vine triggered the sweaty pleasures of adolescence. Yes, that Cornish mother definitely knew what she was talking about.

On my very last day in St. Ives, I discovered a second cluster of honeysuckle vine. I took the path that meandered through the Tregenna Castle grounds to the road leading into the center of town, as I had done all week. I took many photos of all the vegetation growing along the path and texted them to my husband, who identified mallow, fuchsia, St. John's wort, yew trees, geraniums, aucuba, (he thought), English oak and sycamore trees. No honeysuckle.

Then I found it. Surprisingly, I had walked right past the spot several times where it sprawled over a retaining wall beside the road, splaying its last blooms. This one looked tired, mangled and drooping, reflecting the way I had been feeling for the last few days. I was exhausted, running out of breath, as I huffed back up the hill to my Tregenna lodging, with a cough that was getting worse. I wanted to be home, wrapped in a fat duvet, with my husband cuddling me and bringing me cups of tea. If the honeysuckle binds me to my past, to the hot, flower-festooned hideaways of my teenage years, it also winds me back to my husband and the warm comforts of home.

The Church of St. Senara in Zennor

# THE MERMAID, THE CURMUDGEON, THE MAGICIAN AND THE CHURCHYARD

*Laurie McAndish King*

The Mermaid of Zennor was a salacious creature. Flowing hair, a sinuous body, and a bewitching voice were her most obvious attributes, but there were others. She was captivatingly beautiful. She wore no bodice—as is the custom with mermaids—sporting seaweed and pearls to great effect. And she could enchant a man with just her song. That is what happened to poor Matthew Trewhella more than six hundred years ago, at the Church of St. Senara on the wild western coast of Cornwall.

This story has been told and retold for centuries. Surely it is a myth, for mermaids do not exist—do they? Now that I have visited Cornwall, I'm not so sure. It is a remote place, magical and mysterious and home to many stories that tangle truth and legend.

The unfortunate Trewhella fellow was hardly an innocent in the affair. It was his fine tenor voice, singing praises to God in the church choir, and magnified by a particular resonance with Cornwall's cool coastal fog, that first drew the mermaid up from the depths of the sea. She began to appear in the back of the church with unnerving frequency, a long black dress disguising her pale, piscine body. Each Sunday, a small pool of water where the interloper had stood betrayed her presence.

From her position behind the last pew, the mermaid attracted young Matthew's attention.

"Your voice is so beautiful," she may have murmured.

"So you have heard me sing?" I imagine he inquired, a bit disingenuously.

"Yes, I could not resist slipping into the church to hear you sing, even though my home is in the sea and I can only venture out for very short periods of time, lest I forget how to breathe beneath the water," she likely continued—breathlessly, of course.

"And yours ..." he may well have responded, enchanted by her attributes. "I imagine yours must be the voice of an angel. Tell me, are you an angel, come from the sea?"

"I am a mermaid," she surely replied. "Would you like to hear me sing?"

The two soon fell in love, the story goes, as young vocalists often do. They sang to each other from afar. Bit by bit, Matthew's church attendance declined. He frequently traipsed over to nearby Pendour Cove to search for the mermaid. And one day he disappeared.

The boy's father, understandably distraught, endeavored to outwit the lovers and secure his son's return. His plan was to play to the mermaid's conceit, employing the village woodcarver to build a beautiful chair adorned with a portrayal of the mermaid's sensual charm. Everyone knows that mermaids are conceited; that is why they are depicted with a mirror or comb in hand. He situated the chair inside the church. Surely that would lure her back.

But it did not.

"Your father is trying to trick us," the mermaid must have observed.

"I want to be free of his controlling, manipulative ways," the young man surely exclaimed. "I'm never going back again!"

And so the couple remained at their home on the rocky seabed at

Pendour Cove, never again venturing onto land. The chair still sits inside
St. Senara's church in Zennor, a centuries-old reminder of their love,
of the sensuous dangers lurking beneath the sea, and of the mysterious
power of a beautiful voice.

If the mermaid was a myth, the chair is a truth—and I wanted to
see it for myself. Further, if the chair was real, then why relegate the well-
known story of its origin to mythology? Perhaps the mermaid story was
also true.

But the famous Mermaid Chair was impossible to view on the day
I visited Zennor. The church, normally open, was locked. Tony Farrell, a
local historian who was showing me around, was positively chivalrous in
his attempt to get me inside. As it happened, Tony sings in the choir at
St. Senara—perhaps as beautifully as Matthew Trewhella once did. Tony
therefore knew that the key is sometimes kept in the nearby museum,
when no one is available to tend the church, so he set off to fetch it.

But the museum was also closed, and the local volunteer who had
custody of the key had just been rushed to hospital with the flu, so we
had no choice but to retire to Zennor's only pub, The Tinners Arms, to
refresh and regroup.

The pub sits just across a narrow gravel road from St. Senara's. Built
in 1271 to serve the masons and carpenters who came to the area to
construct the church, it hasn't changed much over the years. Its low,
planked ceilings and cold stone floors are surely original. The ambiance
inside is warm, though, and the pub's monumental open hearth is large
enough to accommodate the huge bundles of crackling gorse that have
tindered Cornish fires for centuries.

The Cornish ales there sounded delightful, with names like Tribute,
Doom Bar and Black Prince. But I am not a beer drinker and opted
instead for a whisky, celebrating the fact that Scotland is a mere 600 miles
away. The bartender, a handsome young man in a red-plaid flannel shirt,

seemed unfamiliar with scotches, so Tony recommended the Lagavulin Islay for me and ordered himself a draft of St. Austell.

We sat at the very same table at which D.H. Lawrence once wrote. There were only four tables, and I spent some time at each one, just to be sure. Lawrence lived in Zennor during the Great War years of 1916 and 1917, and lodged briefly at The Tinners Arms while his cottage nearby at Higher Tregerthen was being made ready.

Higher Tregerthen, you may recall, was the home from which Lawrence's flamboyant German wife, Frieda, famously hung her red knickers out on the clothesline, provoking suspicious townspeople to assert that she was sending secret signals to German submarines off the coast and should be forced to move from the town of Zennor. Further cause for suspicion grew from the fact that Frieda was a cousin to the infamous Red Baron, Manfred von Richthofen.

"Oh, to hell vit dem!" Frieda no doubt huffed. "I'll hang my undies vherever I please."

"It's your perfect right, Frieda!" ol' D.H. must have offered. "Let's go sing German folk songs at The Tinners Arms." And so they did.

"Bring along your boyfriend Villiam for good measure," Frieda might have suggested. "That'll get those provincial tongues a-vagging."

"They have got the souls of insects," D.H. is known to have said, referring disparagingly to the locals. Not long afterwards and not surprisingly, the Lawrences received an expulsion order requiring them to leave Cornwall within three days.

Despite his love/hate relationship with Cornwall, D.H. Lawrence was captivated by its mysterious past. "The old race is still revealed, a race which believed in the darkness, in magic ... which is fascinating."

"It is something like King Arthur and Tristan," he wrote. "One can feel free here, for that reason—feel the world as it was in that flicker of pre-Christian Celtic civilization, when humanity was really young ...."

Lawrence was intrigued by his Celtic studies, which were fueled by the early twentieth-century Celtic revivalist movement popular in Cornwall. He even tried to revive the Cornish language, making it a condition of membership in *Rananim*, the community he planned to found as an "anti-national protest against imperialism."

As we settled in at The Tinners Arms, enjoying our liquor and reflecting upon mermaids and Lawrence, I remembered visiting the legendary haunts of King Arthur on the previous afternoon. Camelot, which I had suspected never really existed in King Arthur's day, certainly exists now. It stands proudly on the coast of north Cornwall, in the form of the large and somewhat modern looking (for a castle) Camelot Castle Hotel, serving a luxurious cream tea to tourists along with an invitation "from Arthur" to "write a personal letter to Merlin …"

> *"He is very interested to hear about anything that you need and to hear about any wishes hopes and dreams that you have in any part of life however large or small.*
>
> *"Every letter to Merlin written at this round table will get a personal reply directly from him that you may find extremely valuable, so be sure to include your address or email on the letter and post it in Merlin's letter box …."*

I wrote to Merlin—who wouldn't?—and included both my email and postal addresses for his convenience. I haven't yet received a reply, but that is not a surprise. I can envision the magician in his dark cliff-cave, busily casting spells next to the furious sea. I'm sure he has lots of work to do and he doesn't have the elves, like Santa does, to assist with correspondence.

Down the hill from the Camelot Castle Hotel lies Tintagel. Once a grand fortress, it now disintegrates on the cliffs. Wild grasses encroach on the remnants of Tintagel's stacked-stone gatehouse and wide courtyard, the placid ladies' garden and the Great Hall. Thick gray walls with regularly spaced defensive portals suggest the challenges of medieval life. And Tintagel's ancient vibes—of power and potential, danger and intrigue—are a lasting reminder of the drama of King Arthur's magical conception there.

For me, the ruins of Tintagel, barely extant, conjured ageless truths. My visit had made the old Camelot—in which I had not believed— much more real than the new Camelot, which I had seen with my own eyes. Cornwall was playing tricks with history.

As I sipped my whisky and mused about the tangle of truth and myth, Tony told me about the St. Senara churchyard, which I'd had plenty of time to visit while he hunted for the church key.

"Did you notice the marker, the one about Davey?"

I had seen it. The plaque on a lichen-encrusted exterior wall read:

*To honour the Memory of JOHN DAVEY, of Boswednack in this Parish (b. St. Just, 1812; d. Boswednack, 1891), who was the last to possess any considerable Traditional Knowledge of the Cornish Language & that of his Father & Instructor, JOHN DAVEY, of St. Just (b. Boswednack 1770; d. St. Just 1844), well known as a Mathematician & Schoolmaster, both of whom lie buried near; this Stone was set up by the St. Ives Old Cornwall Society, 1930.*

"John Davey was *not* the last person to speak Cornish fluently," Tony revealed. "It was Jack Mann from Zennor—he lived at about the same time as Davey."

"He lived right here, but didn't get a plaque?" Surely the church knew about him. Zennor (current population: 271) has never been a large town.

"Jack died in 1914, but didn't receive a plaque because of his lowly status as a farm laborer."

I didn't doubt Tony's word. His family has lived in Cornwall for many generations, and his forebears surely would have known both John Davey and Jack Mann.

"That's a sad story."

"Yes, but it's the way the church was," Tony responded.

Could this be true? Had the church really ignored Jack Mann simply because of his lack of status? Would history forget him for the same reason? I wanted to know.

And I had another source. My online informant, Wikipedia, cited Dorothy "Dolly" Pentreath, who died in December 1777, as the last Cornish speaker, even though the same article acknowledged "traditional Cornish speaker John Davey, Junior (d. 1891)" and others, including a "John Mann." So much for clearing up the confusion. The article also mentioned that Dolly was known to curse people, often calling them a name she was particularly fond of: *kronnekyn hager du*—or "ugly black toad." Dolly was said to have been a witch.

What will history remember? Online researchers will find the story about Dolly Pentreath. More rigorous scholars will discover the churchyard documentation about John Davey, Jr. And the stories about Jack Mann? Well, they may one day be lost as the locals grow old, move away, or forget history.

I ordered another Lagavulin and pondered Cornwall's tangled truths.

River in Cornwall

# THE INTERLOPER

*Sandra Bracken*

Slip-sliding down the bank of Pont Creek on a damp morning, an awkward arrival; I beg your pardon, Daphne du Maurier, I hope I am not intruding. Sitting here, all muddied, I see you in a small boat with your parents on your way to Lanteglos Church; it's your wedding day. In another boat, your husband-to-be sits with his parents. He's good-looking. Perhaps that is too personal an observation. Later, in Fowey I look over to Ferryside, your first home in Cornwall—you were over the moon when your family bought that house. I see you there ... writing. That imagined image is compelling, an inspiration in the most straightforward way. Your sense of freedom palpable. Your sense of place fulfilled. Your absorption with your new surroundings complete. Could you be in the throes of creating your novel, *The Loving Spirit*? I know how a place can inspire.

My friend in Polruan, across the harbor and up the hill, says I should move to Cornwall. I love it here, too, but in my heart I feel it belongs to you. You were here first and embraced it so completely. You intuitively knew that Cornwall was right for you. But I, too, know how a place can take hold of a person ... even a foreigner. Being the foreigner, I am the interloper, as your unnamed heroine in *Rebecca* is made to feel an interloper at Manderley, or like the solitary yachtsman in *Frenchman's Creek* who hesitates, senses he is an interloper as he rows upriver from Helston.

I am not so timid. My response to place, like yours, is intuitive and strong. There's not a footstep I take without feeling you have been before me. It's as if you are shadowing me, not the other way around. I follow you and Dona St. Colomb of *Frenchman's Creek* to Navron House on the creek's bank, "a place to drowse and sleep." Together we "lie out in the garden, hour after hour, watching the butterflies as they frolicked in the sun, chased one another, and had their moment; listening to the birds … so busy, so ardent."

What's not to admire about Dona's eagerness to leave her superficial life in London, and her energy, her appetite for the country as she explores the grounds of Navron. And her sensuousness as she discovers a self she did not know.

That new self is found in Cornwall.

Ah, the fantasy … a beguiling place, a seductive pirate, a woman's growing awareness of her powers. When she walks through the field of bluebells going to the river, I'm there. I'm remembering a visit to Lanhydrock, not far from Frenchman's Creek, a stately country house surrounded by gardens, ancient woodlands and riverside paths. I imagine it to be Dona's. I swoon at the memory, crystal clear, of that divine spring day. Well, maybe I'm a bit carried away by Dona's fervor. It's lovely to get lost in her world.

Not so that of Mary Yellon's while she was at *Jamaica Inn*. Oh, yes, I can get caught up in the drama of that dark mysterious world as well, with its hellish circumstances. But I don't want to linger there.

Oh, by the way, those *Birds*. While I'm in awe of your imagination, I'm sorry, I've never had any but the most normal experiences with birds.

Including the obnoxious seagulls of St. Ives. Yes, one shat on my head, but I simply thought I was in the wrong place at the wrong time.

Changing the subject, it's well known that you like walking on alone. I do too. But come walk with me briefly along the southwest coast of Cornwall just beyond the Hayle Estuary, from St. Ives to Gurnard's Head. This shore is different from your verdant southern shore, but these are the places and moments I know best. When you first came to Cornwall you found your Ferryside, then Menabilly, your real-life Manderley.

Morenna in St. Ives is my Ferryside—my place to dream, to write, to draw. My friends' home has been my home every time I returned—my upstairs window looking out to the sea between Carrick and Clodgy Point. Each time I come I find new lands and thoughts to be explored. For me—the hungry visitor—the menu is unlimited. Even the delight of the bracken fern on the coastal path brushing my legs or shoulders depending on the season: unfurling freshly green in June, becoming rusty, tangled tall fronds in October. I venture inland to the rugged gorse and heather-covered high ground on the Lands End Peninsula where the past wraps around me, and each time is new. Time here is marked by *menhir* and *dolmen*. I know the freedom you speak of in your work. I have traveled often and alone. I think you would understand as I carefully pick a gorse blossom and press it into my drawing pad. And I take a handful of luxuriant dark soil, so like charcoal, to use as my drawing material. You use your words so elegantly, so well. I do not. My response to your Cornwall is visceral as well as visual; a traditional drawing is so inadequate. I create mementoes composed from the elements of this day, this time.

Time passes, and I return to a different shore, more than three thousand miles from yours.

I gaze eastward to a salmon sun emerging from the horizon. My house by the sea is not Menabilly, no dramatic headlands and wild ocean waves here. No drama of pirates and smugglers. Or secret rooms or potions for time travel. But then, I can go to your books for that.

Thank you.

The sandy beach is a benign place today, with shallow mesmerizing waves taking my thoughts into the distance.

On the beach at St. Ives

# DRAWN TO WATER

*Maryly Snow*

"There is *nothing*—absolutely nothing—half so much worth doing as simply messing about in boats."

—Kenneth Grahame, *The Wind in the Willows*

Pirates and shipwrecks, lighthouses and lifeboats, I didn't know about these before my trip to Cornwall, but I had assumed the West Coast of England was the geographical sibling of the West Coast of America, a coast that I knew well, her waters the guide by which I've always set my compass. I imagined the Cornish Coast, west-facing like the Pacific Coast, dotted with sandy beaches, rough cliffs, pocked with caves, clusters of large rocks with surging water and waves. I wanted to paddle the jagged coastline in a British kayak, what the Brits call a *canoe*, with their soft chines, narrow beams, and lots of rocker. Of course, I would explore the Cornish Coast.

Before I arrived in St. Ives, I had searched the Internet for kayaking opportunities. I was surprised; I didn't find much—websites touting beginner classes, photos depicting plastic yellow sit-on-tops. I had paddled those in 1993 when I was just a beginner. They're slow and stable, cold and wet; the self-draining scupper holes are the same holes that let in cold water. If I'd had any doubts about the salty ocean siblings, the water temperature of the Celtic Sea truly makes it the sister of the Northern Pacific: cold. Plus, I didn't want a class. I wanted an outing, an adventure.

Online, I learned about Cornish *coasteering*, jumping from rocks into the frigid water. It looked like exhilarating, cold fun for someone younger and more agile than I. I wanted to be gliding by cliffs and rocks, feeling waves surge, hearing the swoosh and clapotis of water, my kayak sliding up close to, then down from sea-mossed and barnacled rocks. Mostly, I dreamed of paddling through wave crests, slip-sliding with the water, water that had the potential to smash my boat, water that can just as easily be my friend, rocking endlessly gentle.

I heard the surge of ocean in my waking dreams, imagined its motion beneath me. Surely, I could find something better than a sit-on-top introductory paddle. It's only in hindsight that I realized my mistake: I should have searched for English *canoeing*.

The train rides to Cornwall—from London to St. Erth and St. Erth to St. Ives—were easy and gorgeous with the English countryside, small pastures crossed by three-hundred-year-old rock hedgerows on one side, the ocean on the other. Once in St. Ives, the ocean's call grew stronger. After I walked from Tregenna Castle downhill to the harbor, I heard a booming voice hawking three boat trips a day: fishing in the morning, Godrevy Lighthouse mid-day, Seal Islands late afternoon.

I was just in time for the *Seahorse*'s afternoon run and my first excursion on the Cornish Sea. With five other passengers, I climbed aboard the open-air boat from a causeway near Smeaton's Pier. Soon, on the open ocean, with sea-wind-ruffled salty hair, I watched a pod of bottlenose dolphins charm us: bow-surfing, porpoising alongside, cavorting as if showing off. Then, as we edged-in close to Seal Islands, really just a cluster of rocks, I delighted in watching two enormous sea lions bob in the surge, hanging tail down, only their noses visible.

A few days later, on a trip to the harbor town of Fowey, I impulsively hopped on an open-air launch for a boat tour. After greeting the other four passengers, all English, I watched the captain repeatedly shovel something from a storage bin into a fire. Coal! I was astonished to find myself on a quaint, putt-putting, coal-fired steam launch. As we chugged along the edge of town toward the sea, five row houses as colorful as San Francisco's famed Painted Ladies came into view. The captain pointed toward a mansion behind them: It was the majestic Fowey Hall Hotel, the inspiration for Toad Hall in the *The Wind in the Willows*.

Suddenly he turned away from my heart's desire to cross the Fowey Estuary to Polruan, the village on the other side. I sputtered out my question.

"Nay, it's too rough today for the open ocean," he replied.

I looked longingly over my shoulder toward the sea and the mouth of the estuary while we chugged upriver. We passed author Daphne du Maurier's childhood home, Ferryside. Then we came upon the startling Fowey China Clay Docks, behemoth loading docks, eerily silent, consistently gray, not a soul in sight, making it hard to imagine the tremendous volume of china clay that is still exported from Fowey. I've since heard that the river presents excellent kayaking—I mean canoeing—opportunities upstream.

For my next water excursions, I owe Jeff. I'd met this handsome Cornishman in San Francisco years before when he had been welcomed into my kayaking club. Now, in exchange, he hosted me at his. On our agreed-upon day, Jeff picked me up from my cottage at Tregenna Castle and drove me to the Hayle Canoe Club: four shipping containers along the edge of the Hayle River. There he assembled a kit that would fit me: kayak, paddle, pfd (personal floatation device or life-jacket), and a paddle jacket to keep me dry. Once kitted-out, we paddled down the Hayle toward St. Ives Bay. Ahead of us, the smallest rows of gently spilling waves beckoned. Jeff motioned for me to stop. "We can't go any further," he said. "The tide is ebbing. Straight ahead there are sandbars across the mouth of the river. With the tide going out, we'd be stuck on any one of 'em for hours, from noon to night."

I tried to hide my disappointment with my voice. "Oh, right," I replied cheerfully. So we turned around and paddled up and down the gentle river for our trial run.

Undaunted, I was still eager for the ocean. The next day Jeff and I made the long, sun-dappled drive to Falmouth. There we met Doug, keeper of the keys, and two newer members of the Hayle Canoe Club. The five of us easily launched from the funky, friendly Loe Beach on the Fal River and paddled away from the ocean, because—as Jeff said—"the best British summer in recent history has reverted to its windy, gusting, white-capped self."

Green hillsides protected us from the wind. We passed the historic and still thatched Smugglers Inn and the stately Tregothnan manse, England's only tea plantation.

We glided by three monstrous container ships moored in the center of the river. Persistent wind coupled with Cornish accents and local idioms made hearing and comprehending difficult. I struggled to understand my paddling partners. Still, I gleaned multiple explanations for the hulking vessels: The ghost ships didn't meet the EU's health and safety rules; their true owners were impossible to trace; the crews were virtual prisoners, having neither passports nor money; the global shipping trade had plummeted.

All very interesting, but I still hadn't made it to the ocean.

My obsession with the ocean continued unabated. I prowled the St. Ives Lifeboat Station. I took an AirBnB with a harbor view. I tried to catch the *Seahorse* for its Godrevy run (too rough both times), kept my ears tuned for every utterance of the word *mermaid*.

I never saw the Mermaid of Zennor, but I did meet the *Mermice of Mousehole* at St. Ives Booksellers, ate salt-water fish whenever possible, and always asked for Moo-Maid Ice Cream.

Of course, none of these substitutes quite satisfied, even though they occupied me. And I've learned my lesson. For my next visit to Cornwall, I'll arrange for ocean canoeing well in advance, will paddle much further up the Fal, hope for less windy days, and might even attempt *coasteering*.

Lidded pot by David Leach

# PAUL'S PRECIOUS POT

*Ethel Mussen*

In Cornwall, the local gods and goddesses are Daphne du Maurier, Barbara Hepworth, Bernard Leach and John Wesley. Three were creative artists, one was a preacher, and all have left legacies in this peninsular community. And all were "foreigners" who invaded and imprinted their lives, works and philosophies on the insular people who live here and consider themselves a separate country from England. As a collector of ceramics, I came to St. Ives to discover what I could about the world-renowned potter, Bernard Leach. My husband had proudly acquired a Leach lidded pot many years ago, but I had known little of its history or importance. This was my singular opportunity to learn about it, first hand, at the Leach Museum and workshop.

Collectors don't explain to each other "why" they collect, but "what." The drive to acquire is a given. For my husband, Paul, and me it was subsumed in his proposal, as he cupped his hands around the copper mug of ginger beer and vodka—Scandia's Moscow Mule—and barely looking at me, confessed that he thought, "We could make a beautiful life together."

I leaned forward and patted his hand and agreed that I thought so, too. No words of love were spoken, but after a summer of deliberate separation, we both recognized that life together might be richer than if we continued alone in our academic careers. To affirm our commitment, the next day we went to Laguna Beach and bought an inexpensive but attractive hemp hanging, silkscreened with green fish. That morning, Paul had blanched at the sight of the marquise diamond ring my uncle displayed for us. Even wholesale diamonds were off limits to this socialist ideologue who scorned personal decoration as obnoxious bourgeois aggrandizement. However, the twelve-inch-high Tang horse we found in Chinatown the next day was deemed compatible with the hanging for our Columbus, Ohio, apartment.

When we returned to Columbus, we pooled our previous framed acquisitions—his Diego Rivera reproduction of the *Calla Lily Vendor* and my museum print of Picasso's *Olga—Woman in White*. Add Paul's three small Mexican serapes and three Balinese figurines, and our marriage on the walls was prefigured. To make up for the diamond, Paul brought a pair of Navajo channel-work silver and turquoise earrings from Denver, where he had stopped to work on the textbook he was writing in collaboration with a former Yale classmate. It was the first of several settings of turquoise and silver and other semi-precious sets that were more acceptable decoration for the professor's wife. I knew that I would never have the engagement diamond I had always expected, but settled instead for the objects of beauty or interest that we found wherever we traveled.

The textbook was a financial and academic success and brought many invitations to campuses throughout the United States and other parts of the world. Ethnic arts—expressions of religions and mythology from different cultures—brought the works of many hands onto our shelves. Prints, etchings and paintings by famous or local artists colored the walls. His, mine, and ours distinguished the variety of our collections which focused later on glass—(ours) and ceramics—(mine). Whenever possible, we bought from the artists themselves. Aside from knowing the backstory of many lives, I treasured touching the hands that created the art. In Bali, the carver boasted that his karma was transferred to me when I bought the mask he'd crafted. I realized that this seemed true for every piece we owned. It was not only the aesthetic beauty, but the soul of the artist and the culture of his society that we shared when we added a work.

Now, in October, 2014, I traveled with other writers to St. Ives. Paul had died in 2000, but this trip gave me an opportunity to learn about one of his acquisitions. Its background had long been a mystery to me, even though Paul had announced triumphantly that it was a Leach pot. It was about six inches high, similar to a small tea caddy. A lid settled comfortably on the high shoulders of the body, which glowed in a light taupe glaze. A fernlike design was painted on one side in a warm brown, supposedly by Bernard himself. I hadn't known of Leach before, in spite of the fact that I was the collector of ceramics. When I later heard his name, I felt comfort in knowing we had a piece of his work. For years, however, it rested only partially visible among several objects in a display cabinet near the fireplace, but I forgot where Paul had obtained it or when, and, of course, I could not ask him now. In Cornwall, where it had been crafted, I was ashamed of my ignorance and sought its story at the source.

My assumption was that so many artists had gravitated to Cornwall because of the prevalence of earthly elements—metal, clay, sand—and a creative community. Pottery and glass shops prospered in the village. Clay pits and tin mines were touted tourist trips. Hepworth, the sculptor, and Leach, the potter, had museums of their own, and the Tate branch displayed the work of both. So I took the taxi to the upper limit of town on Higher Stennack Road to the Leach Pottery and museum. Guy, the cheery guard/greeter, kindly permitted me to browse through the biographical books at his desk before I began my tour.

Bernard was born in 1887 in Hong Kong where his father was a British diplomat. His mother died at his birth, however, and he shuttled back and forth between his father in Asia and his grandparents in England, where he met his cousin, Muriel Coyle. He studied engineering and etching skills in England and then returned to Japan to blend English and Japanese artistic techniques. He married the docile Muriel and spent more years in Japan, but was intent on introducing this unique blend in England. He joined some other potters in a country community and persuaded a Japanese friend, Hamada Shōji, to come with him. Although his family had grown to four sons and a daughter, his marriage to Muriel dissolved. A charismatic womanizer and visionary establishing a "Creative Community," he was given land just outside of St. Ives, together with a livable stipend by a wealthy patroness, Mrs. Horne. In 1920, he and Hamada built their pottery on High Stannack Road. Serendipity and financial stability determined the location. The china clay happened to be near, but was not recognized as an asset at the beginning.

His international fame and presence had already brought an entourage, a brief second marriage to a secretarial assistant, and a third wife, Janet Trannell, who came from America to study and then to wed. With Muriel's death, the sons and daughters also joined him. Sons, David and Michael, and son-in-law, Dicon, were active potters and improvers of kilns, turning wheels, and manufacturing practices to support the studio art production.

Guy explained that the display before me was a compendium of Leach pots and that a map would help me through the self-guided tour of the original pottery rooms, passing to the present pottery. Signage was explicit and the creator of each pot was identified as Bernard Leach or his wife or a son, or Hamada and the other Japanese artists who had come for some years and worked with Bernard. The wall displays were lined with large and small examples of pots and plates from many different years. Just opposite the reception desk, however, was an array of Leach and Hamada wares. The glazes and decorations were grays and browns with swirling brushwork in some that echoed the abstract leaves on our pot. None were lidded, however; all were open-throated vases and ewers. The years were so varied that I could not place ours in context, yet they were related in decoration. I could henceforth cite the Japanese influence.

At a gallery in town I had seen pots and vases for sale attributed to Janet and Michael Leach or an apprentice. Now I knew that Janet was Bernard's third wife. I thought about the long-suffering Muriel. Like other artist's wives I'd known, these first mates seem to foster the young creative ego, then live at home to raise the offspring while the exuberant male seeks further excitement and variety with other women in a broader world. Muriel spawned five potters among sons and grandsons to carry on the trade and eventually create the foundation. John, the youngest, now lived and potted in Somerset, but visited St. Ives to oversee production and the general status of the existing foundation. The pottery had closed in 2005 when eldest son, David, had died, but was revived later to produce what was called "standard" tableware. Bernard had envisioned accessible tableware for "ordinary" Englishmen instead of the delicate tea wares of English porcelain. Not only would it be homey and sturdy, much like other European earthenware, but he hoped its popularity would support the studio or "art" pottery. Now it supported the museum itself.

When Bernard and his friend, Hamada, developed the pottery, they built a small manageable workshop in contrast to the large famous English industries of Staffordshire such as Coalport and Wedgewood. Like Barbara Hepworth, who later joined the community, they brought craftsmanship and individual artistry to Cornwall. Messy marriages seemed to come with the Cornish air and carry a cachet of free love that inspired free creation. If the preserved kilns and samples of clay exhibited in the adjoining rooms reminded us of manufacture, the entryway portrait of an elderly Bernard in 1972, lovingly trimming the lip of a damp vase, brought to life the presence of the man forming the pot. When Paul picked his pot, he had a good eye for design and a feel for the fame of the maker. I hold it and feel the turn of the wrist in the swirl of the rabbit's fur brush laying down the leaves just so, and the thin line of orange defining the edge of the lid. I honor the craft and empathize with the entrepreneur who produces inspiration and also everyday wares to support his existence.

Eventually I reached the salesroom with pots and bowls by several contemporary workers. Standard wares and art intermingled. Among them was a table of works by Amanda Brier, who had worked at the pottery until 2005 when it closed. Even though she has her own studio at Falmouth, she is presently director of education for the Leach Pottery and runs an active children's program offered by the foundation.

One of her vases caught me in my collector's heart. Pale aqua, about six inches high, and turned with a swirling form at the shoulder, I felt this was waiting for me as a modern legacy by another woman Bernard would have admired had he lived to mentor her. I confided in the rosy woman who wrapped this vase that I had Paul's pot at home. I now knew from seeing the museum's display that it was clearly decorated in the Leach-Hamada style, but I didn't know for sure who made it.

"There'll be an LB, if it's Bernard, near a small incised seal on the bottom rim."

I was pleased with the day's education and the tip. Now I could go home with new information and a new pot of my own.

Before leaving England I made one final stop at the Victoria and Albert Museum to see if they included Bernard Leach in the history of English ceramics. Samples of ancient Greek and Roman pots were displayed on the left wall followed by Asian. Later examples from

European centers were visible across the room. Two vitrines were devoted to Bernard Leach as the progenitor of the Contemporary English School of stoneware and earthenware. The rest of the historical areas were minimal samples of what I knew were the museum's vast collections of English earthenware and porcelain of the eighteenth and nineteenth centuries. This timeline was only a suggestion, but it did enshrine Leach by name and place. Paul would have expected this recognition.

Home again in Berkeley, nine days after my visit to the Leach Pottery, I unpacked my blue Brier vase and set it beside the lidded pot. Quivering, I turned over the pot and found the seal and LD, for David, not Bernard. That David made this suggests that the lid is a stylistic successor to the earlier open pitchers and that it borders on the practical usefulness of the standard wares. Amanda's pot is pure artwork and does not pair comfortably with David's. They are two different generations of color and form so I display them on top of the cabinet, slightly apart. But I still cherish each—understanding and relishing their separate histories and souls.

One of many uphill climbs in St. Ives

# Uphill all the Way

*Sandra Bracken*

A vertical trek
and easy to get lost
in the tangle of streets
that go up
from Downalong.
Easier to follow
random streets up
than try to make sense
of the way.
Reaching Salubrious Place
I've gone too far
in the wrong direction.
The only sure way
not to get lost is
walk along
Porthmeor Beach
Before undertaking
the path
through the graveyard

a scenic route.
Barnoon,
cemetery with a view,
has grassy places for resting.
I pause
and look
for the famous headstone
faced with ceramic tiles.
Through the iron gate
in the upper wall
a right turn
and more hill ahead.
I can almost see
Clodgy Point.
Glad to turn onto
a level street
and again
at Carthew Terrace.
At last
my destination
and more
steps to
climb.

Modern bonfires, ancient rituals

# THE TIME-TRAVELER:
# A TALE OF TWO COUNTRIES

*Joanna Biggar*

I am in a small stone church near the sea in Zennor, Cornwall. It is humble, plain, haunting. In early autumn, the parishioners are festooning it with sheaves of wheat and preparing to celebrate harvest and the "Crying of the Neck," when the last ear of corn is picked.

I am searching here for connections to St. Senara for whom this church is named. Beneath the medieval stones of the fifteenth-century church, I imagine the bones of another, dating from the sixth century. That is when Senara, a Breton princess, and a woman said to have had a "dubious reputation," married a Breton king. Perhaps bewitched by her, but also influenced by the gossip she attracted, he accused her of adultery when she became pregnant. He cast her into the sea in a barrel. At sea, she was visited by an angel, converted to Christianity, and gave birth to a son in the waves. They washed up on land in Cornwall, where she founded Zennor and the church that took her name. Her son was to become St. Budoc, a bishop of Ireland, and both their names were added to a large roster of Celtic saints who are recognized only in Celtic lands, including Cornwall and Brittany.

My curiosity aroused by this tale, and by the ties between these two outposts of Celtic culture—both descendants of the mythical King

Arthur and separated by English Channel—I wonder how the ancient ways have survived in each "country." For beneath their distinctive black and white "national" flags, they claim they are Cornish or Breton first, before being English or French.

Leaving the church I stumble, my foot catching an old gravestone. When I stand upright again, I am on a hillside outside Zennor.

*Crowds of people, many disguised by long robes and covered faces, weave and dance before an enormous bonfire. In the firelight I see the silhouettes of nine standing stones in a circle. An unseen voice makes itself understood to me in a Celtic tongue, explaining that the place is called the Nine Sisters.*

*"You have come at the liminal time," it continues, "when the spirits and the fairies can move more easily between worlds."*

*I come to understand the voice is one such spirit. It seems my foot has fallen through a crack in time. "Now we must bring the animals down from summer pastures, choose some for slaughter and prepare for winter," it says. "Now, too, the dead move among us and dine with us tonight. Look into any hut and you will see the place laid. Tonight all the old fires from each hearth are extinguished to be rekindled by the new bonfire."*

*Amazed, I watch mummers, maskers and musicians, and diviners making predictions from apple peels and roasted nuts. It is October 31st, and the Celtic celebration of Samhain fills the Cornish sky with fire and song and the shadows of the spirits.*

I trip again and I am back at St. Senara's Church. My guide is Tony Farrell, whose roots here twist back to the time of the ancient bonfires. A tall, imposing man with a mop of grayish curls and eyes that reflect the blue of the sea, he combines all the elements of Cornwall passed down from generations of fishermen, seamen and miners. An archeologist, English teacher and poet, he uses his voice as an instrument to play the story of Cornwall—in all its beauty, humor and melancholy.

"To me being Celtic is being Cornish and being Cornish is being not English," he says. A graduate of Trinity University, Belfast, he adds, smiling wickedly, "I didn't want to go to university in England—it's an alien country."

So, what, I ask Tony, is this fiercely held identity that makes one Cornish? As we skirt the moors in the last blooms of heather, squeeze past narrow hedgerows and cultivated green fields, and follow the rock-strewn coast, the restless sea, he answers. These are the basic elements: language, a strong musical tradition, and a shared history with ancient family ties.

Of all the extant Celtic lands, only in Cornwall did the language die—they say with an eighteenth-century fishwife, the last fully "native" speaker. But it began disappearing under the Tudor King Henry VIII, who introduced Anglicanism—anathema to the Catholic Cornish—and whose son continued his reforms by imposing the *Book of Common Prayer* in English. An uproar followed, leading to an uprising, the Prayer Book Rebellion, whose casualties included several thousand dead on the battlefield—and eventually, Tony explains, without a Cornish Bible, the Cornish language.

A renewed interest in all things Celtic that began in the nineteenth century, however, resulted in a revivalist movement in Cornwall, including Cornish. The language has been reconstructed—much of it based on Welsh and especially Breton. Speakers can be found in pubs and little classrooms learning to speak the language of their forebears.

Yet despite Cornwall's official status of separate national identity, and recognition of Cornish from the Council of Europe and the UK government as a Regional Minority Language, there are few speakers and too little funding. It's part of the Celtic Revival, Tony declares, which was very strong twenty years ago. "Bonfires every summer on hilltops, singing in Penzance. In Helston, in May, thousands dance the Flora Dance and men get themselves up in morning suits and top hats and everybody gets hammered ..."

He pauses, then sums up by quoting his late father, a fisherman, about righting this old wrong: "Bugger the label, just give us the money."

As for where Cornish music is now, he says, it can be found, transformed, where the real Cornish folk are—inside Methodist Churches. When John Wesley came to Cornwall in the eighteenth century, his message of hope and instant salvation found an eager audience in this rocky country of poor and marginalized miners, seafarers and fishermen. He came thirty-two times and drew crowds of up to 20,000. But because folk music was associated with drinking and pubs, it was forbidden by the Methodists, and the Cornish poured their souls into chord singing and hymns instead.

I am in front of the boat-strewn harbor in the village of St. Ives.

*A parade of musicians from centuries past, some in kilts, passes me, playing fiddles, bagpipes and harps; many are dancing. They turn a corner and I follow, only to blink and find myself inside modern day Fore Street Methodist Church. The walls are festooned with blue and white nets. Behind the altar is the sign of the fish, signifying Christ, and the musicians, now sitting in pews facing it, bob their heads (many of them white) as they sing, their rich harmonies blending into a single voice. "Oh, Lord, give me an undivided heart."*

Across the Channel some days later, I am standing in the school-yard of the Skol Diwan, in the tiny town named Plournaz in Northern Brittany. Grade-school-aged children run, shout and play under cloudy Breton skies, which occasionally release streams of rain. But the twenty-five children in this immersion school pay no attention, nor does their pretty, young teacher, Claire Klurve. She is enthusiastic about being here.

Having learned Breton from her parents, she caught the revivalist fervor of keeping the old ways and language alive. "The culture is still living," she explains to me in French, "even if the language and Breton songs are not sponsored by the government."

The Diwan schools began in 1977 and are supported largely by parents who want their children to learn Breton. Teacher and principal, Joel Donnart, who learned Breton in summers from his grandfather and came to embrace his roots, adds that teaching culture is important, too. "We stress music, dance and cuisine such as salted butter, from the days when Brittany won exemption from the salt tax."

Once inside his class, the kids settle down and are happy to perform for a visitor.

"*An bleiz Kozh*," they begin,

"It's rap," Donnart explains.

My vision shifts again.

*Suddenly I am in crowd in Lorient, Southern Brittany, at the summertime Interceltic Festival, now in its forty-fourth year. Kilt-wearing pipers, costumed drummers and fiddlers march, weave and dance down the street. I am startled to see the faces of the children from Plournanz, singing. Their words are in a local dialect of Breton called cornouaille, or Cornwall. Peeling off into the crowd, they disappear beneath the tall lace headdresses and aprons, bright embroidered jackets and black hats of their forebears.*

I blink and realize I am back near Paimpol overlooking the bay with treacherous rocks, and alive with boats, fishermen and shellfish. The house belongs to my host, guide and friend, Hervé Guilbaud. He is a fit, athletic man, with silver hair, a wicked sense of humor, and eyes that reflect the blue of the sea. A sailor, by inclination, who loves frequent dips off the rocky beach, he is by profession a journalist and writer forced to live in Paris—"*chez les dingues*" (with the crazy people) he says often. Whenever possible, he retreats home to Brittany, where his roots twist back to the time when Celtic Britons began crossing the Channel.

Asked about his Breton identity, he answers: "It has to do with our own history and traditions—we only joined France, you know, in the fifteenth century. But it also has to do with being linked to the sea— many navigators come from Brittany and over 80 percent of the Navy are Breton. Unfortunately it stops short of the language."

Although the language is crucial, its decline has been precipitous: From some 1,000,000 in 1950, only around 200,000 speakers remain now. Hervé says that his grandmother, who wore a traditional lace headdress, spoke Breton as her native tongue. "But then in my grandparents' generation it became forbidden. If somebody spoke it in school, they were made to wear cowbells. We were a poor people living in harsh conditions and made to feel like second-class citizens. It was classy to speak French. Now if you speak Breton in the market, people would call the *gendarmes*."

He grew up with other traditions, too, such as the tale of "*l'Ankou*," a horseman of death who rides through the country and selects people; and the "*Fest Noz*," a summer night festival where "we would dance to chants—and everybody drank a lot." He also had a Jesuit education and grew up Catholic. Brittany remains Catholic, but the influence of the church has vastly waned, As for traditions and festivals, they still continue too, but with fewer people.

Hervé laments this. He applauds the idea of Celtic/Breton Revival, especially the language. "I think one shouldn't get away from the traditions; I think they should be encouraged," he says.

I realize what I hear in Brittany is what I heard in Cornwall. In both these poor and beautiful lands heavily dependent on the sea, Cornish and Bretons have felt marginalized and left behind on their distant peninsulas.

But they remain independent and proud. Despite a loss of old ways and an influx of outsiders, both regions have experienced an interest in revival, which is especially expressed in great pan-Celtic festivals that attract thousands, and in attempts to rekindle their languages, all without government support.

Still, I wonder. What importance could the distant past really have, for example, to Bretons living in the twenty-first century? I mean to ask Hervé.

*Suddenly I am whirling through space and come to a soft landing in a deep forest. It is Bocéliande, deep in Brittany. Oaks and streams abound and I take shelter under a huge, moss-covered beech. From the mists I see knights bearing standards from King Arthur's Round Table. Nine giant standing stones appear in front of me, and barely visible behind one, there is a couple embracing. Creeping closer, I discover the magician, Merlin, who like Arthur, has migrated here from his birthplace in Tintagel, Cornwall. Their voices become clear: The fairy, Viviane, is enticing Merlin to teach her his secrets.*

*I whirl again, blinking, finding myself in another time—my own. Brocéliande has become the Forest of Paimpont. The nine great stones have fallen and only two smaller ones remain, leaning toward each other like lovers. It is Merlin's Tomb, where "trapped in air" by Viviane after she learned his magic, he remains forever, a living spirit. On the red path behind me, I see people: kids in sneakers with backpacks, a young couple holding a baby, a middle-aged man with a bouquet. Creeping closer to the stones I discover tucked in crevices, paper messages, pleas, gifts, votives, prayers—all signs of a people who still believe in the power of the past, all appeals for help from the still-powerful Merlin.*

Ravens atop Tregenna Castle

# THE BIRDS

*Daphne Beyers*

I first saw them standing in rows along the Serpentine in Hyde Park. Their beady, black eyes locked on me as I strode by, long necks swiveling as I passed. People, oblivious, took pictures, threw breadcrumbs, let their children laugh and play in their midst.

A flock of crows is called a murder, but in London, the crows weren't the only birds with murder in their hearts. The waterfowl stood uncannily still and watchful as I passed. Still as only a predator can be still, waiting, watching for weakness, for an opening to stick a beak in.

At first, I, too, dismissed my qualms. These were just birds after all, our feathered friends. Geese, ducks, swans, harmless, the lot of them. Sure, they could honk at you, maybe give you a hard peck on the thigh, but murder? That's going too far, or so I thought.

The gray heron gave me pause, even in those early days. It stood with its long neck tucked in, the shoulders of its wings shrugged high behind its head like Bela Lugosi in a Dracula cape. The gray bird gazed at me with cool disinterest, like it could pick out my intestines as easily as a fish from the lake. I hurried on.

It's the jet lag, I told myself. Exhaustion turning to paranoia. The birds acted odd because they were half-tame from years, decades, of being fed breadcrumbs by London's tourists. Still, they were everywhere: pigeons, seagulls, white cranes from Africa, geese from the Russian Steppes, day birds, night birds, loons. If they ever turned on us … I pushed the thought away, but that night I locked my window and drew the blinds. In the wee hours, I woke to the sound of something cooing softly.

I had intended to stay in London longer, see some sights, until I learned about the seven denizens of the Tower. The Deadly Seven they are sometimes called, the Seven of the Tower, the Black Ravens of Doom. I could see them in my mind's eye, seven fat ravens well fed on raw meat, sitting in the very heart of London like spiders in a web, sending out signals and commands unnoticed by their human minders. I couldn't get out of London fast enough and caught the early train to Cornwall.

The train ride was uneventful, though I did notice crows at every station stop. Were they the same crows or new ones? How could I tell? They all look alike. They could be following me, and I'd never know it.

The fresh sea air of St. Ives was good for me. There did seem to be a lot of seagulls about, but they looked less menacing than the London birds. Three hundred miles from London, I'd gotten out of the radius of the Deadly Seven and could breathe easier.

The first attack came a day later.

I had bought fish and chips from a local store and decided to eat them on the quay. The bird came out of nowhere. I never saw it until it smashed into my left shoulder, almost knocking me to the ground. I caught my balance and my fish and chips and spun to face my attacker. The bird was gone, but five seagulls, two white and three brown, stood in front of me, cooing innocently. I was not fooled. It had been one of them or an accomplice that had flown away.

A passing constable refused to write down my report. He pointed irritably at a sign that read, "Beware the Seagulls" and another that read, "The management is NOT responsible for the wildlife" and stalked away.

"Tourists feeding them," a local woman sniffed and kept going, not batting an eyelid at my bruised shoulder blade.

It wasn't my fish and chips they were after. It was me. The fools thought they were safe if they didn't eat fish and chips on the quay. That seagull had been out for blood, not fried potatoes.

I hurried back to my hotel and searched the Internet for other bird incidents. A search in Cornwall revealed the most horrifying story. Cornish writer Daphne du Maurier had published a short story in 1952 about exactly such an attack entitled, "The Apple Tree," later retitled, "The Birds." In the story, vicious flocks of birds turned on humanity. It was written as a fictional account, but I suspected the truth.

A further search led me to a 1963 movie by Alfred Hitchcock titled, "The Birds," loosely based on Daphne du Maurier's story. In the movie, birds pecked out people's eyes and took over the planet. Hitchcock's movie was also presented as fiction, but I recognized the secret warning.

The birds! It was happening again, sixty years later. I thought I'd escaped the worst of it by fleeing London, but the birds had driven me right to the heart of their uprising: the Cornish Coast. Beautiful, idyllic Cornwall with its sandy beaches and resort-town restaurants had turned into a nightmare of fluttering wings and sharp, piercing beaks. And I, their haunted, driven prey.

I warned the others. No one believed me. Even after a seagull took an ice-cream cone right out of a woman's hand. I watched them gather in great flocks over the moors, those empty places inhospitable to humans and cows alike. White gulls and black birds and every color of bird in-between gathered on those lonely moors to plot and plan. I thought I heard one of their number, a blackbird, crow or jackdaw—I couldn't tell—mutter to itself as it flew past, perhaps reciting a litany or memorizing a battle chant.

There was no escaping them. Even when I climbed the highest cliff on the northern coast, a seagull stood waiting for me. It propped on one leg and opened its beak as if to say, "There is nowhere we can't find you." I cried and shooed it away, but the gull didn't budge from its perch. It stared back at me with cold, defiant eyes.

Days passed. The expected attack didn't come. The birds were playing a long game, trying to weaken me with sleepless nights and the exhaustion of constant vigilance. Or maybe that's the secret to holding off the attack. As long as one of our number knows what they are up to, they'll wait and bide their time.

With a shock I realized that was the purpose behind Hitchcock's movie and du Maurier's story. It wasn't to warn humanity. It was to let the birds know that we knew. But Hitchcock and Daphne du Maurier were both gone. It was up to me.

Birds are descended from dinosaurs. Once they ruled the earth. They've been patient all these millennia, watching from on high as small mammals grew and multiplied and took over their once vast domain. I fear their time has come round at last. There are many more of them than there are of us. They are legion. And far off in the Tower of London, the Seven wait for a sign, some signal of our weakness only their dark eyes can perceive. But I am watching too.

Someday, I know, I'll have to sleep. One of these days, I'll close my eyes too long and that will be the end of the human race.

As I write this, my eyelids droop closed for just a moment. One minute of sleep. That's all I need. I doze off, followed down into dreams by dark eyes and the flutter of wings.

Tintagel Castle ruins

# A BRIEF AND SHINING SPOT

*Unity Barry*

I wanted to find the remnants of Manderley. In truth, I wanted to find the centuries-old mansion, Menabilly, that Daphne du Maurier lived in and used as the model for her masterpiece novel, *Rebecca*. Set in Cornwall, the location reverberated in my mind like the melodramatic mystery movie Alfred Hitchcock made from it in 1940.

Daphne du Maurier had trapped the essence of the land and its people in novels beloved by aficionados of bleak thrillers, like myself. Her stories also captured the imagination of Hollywood filmmakers who distilled her romantic tale of a malevolent spirit in *Rebecca*, or of twisted truths in *My Cousin Rachel*, sending flickers of shadow and mystery across the world's cinema screens. I had recently revisited these black and white classics, so the image of craggy rocks bombarded by angry Atlantic storms saturated the theater of my mind. I envisioned meeting some of the purportedly dour Cornish population, clannish and isolated from the modern world, just like the taciturn and evil antagonist, Mrs. Danvers, in *Rebecca*.

A woman alone, I had arrived late at night following a month-long sojourn in the repressive summer heat and humidity of Barcelona and the baking dryness of Marrakech. I longed for the harsh autumn storms of the rugged Cornish coast, notorious for dense fogs and ocean gales that flogged the cliffs with relentless ferocity. I hoped to watch roiling clouds lash the landscape with torrents of rain, providing my own inspirational backdrop for dark intrigue.

In anticipation of many weeks in wildly differing climates, I had packed a suitcase large enough to stow at least a St. Bernard, maybe even a small pony. At the St. Ives train station, kind passengers helped me unload my cargo down the meter-high drop to the platform, euphemistically called the "gap." Since no cover sheltered the walkway, even in the dark I could see a daunting cliff looming ahead. Supposedly cabs abounded nearby, but nary a one appeared when I needed it most. With no other choice, I wheeled my ridiculously heavy bag up a street that tilted at a jaw-dropping angle then down another hill of an equally acute slant, my trailing luggage threatening to push me, like a toboggan, over the granite paving stones to the distant bottom. Still seeing no cars for hire, I stopped a passing man to ask directions. Shorter than I and very round, he peered at up through his glasses in myopic curiosity, then responded with enthusiasm.

"Ah, me lovely lady, you'll be wanting the taxi rank. Jus' come with me," he volunteered, while wresting my monstrous luggage from my quickly blistering hands. He indicated that I should follow him along a dimly lit narrow lane. Why my American big-city-self-preservation instincts didn't set off warning bells, I'll never know. At home in San Francisco, the eleven o'clock news would surely report the certain disappearance of any woman, new in town and foolish enough to accompany a complete stranger down a dark alley. But as this kindly gnome chatted away in friendly fashion, my worries evaporated, my first Cornishman by no means the dark and dangerous rogue of my expectations.

Once found, a local cab whisked me toward my hotel. The driver proved equally kind and approachable. When I told him I was part of a travel writers' workshop, seeking inspiration from his village, he reached for the book beside him,

"You be a writer, you say? Do you know this?"

He mentioned an author unknown to me and held up a small clothbound book, its title impossible to read in the dim car interior. "One of our own Cornish tin miners wrote it in 1914 about how he left here and went to Australia."

As we drove along the twisting lanes to the top of the hill where my hotel overlooked the sea, the driver recounted with verve the rough-and-tumble exploits of his countryman from another era. He left me with my first hint at how history pervades the local genetic makeup.

The next morning, instead of gloom, I awoke to the cacophony of gulls. Sunshine streamed in the window of my room at the Tregenna Castle Hotel. Construction of the building had started in the late eighteenth century as a private residence, but the structure didn't attain its present ninety-room resort form until 1932. After a hearty, but artery-clogging English breakfast of fried eggs, grilled tomatoes, baked beans, bacon *and* sausages, I grabbed my camera and began exploring the grounds.

The early morning sun turned the golf course grass into brilliant chartreuse under a glittering blanket of dew. Cobalt filled the distant ocean expanse, and above that a vast blue dome with cotton-ball clouds drifted toward shore. Surrounded by acres of scenic woods and lush sub-tropical gardens that thrive in the temperate climate of England's most southern region, the stone hotel sported a crenellated roofline and red ivy-covered walls. I hiked comfortably without even a sweater, feeling as if I walked through the movie set of Sherwood Forest. No dead trees tried to snag my clothes; no brutal gale laden with sea salt lashed my face; no crumbling rocks threatened my steps. Instead it seemed as if Robin Hood, played by a green tights-wearing Errol Flynn, might emerge from the bracken at any moment. I half expected to hear a directorial, "Cut!" and to see studio lights dim to show the dismal landscape of my preconceptions.

A short distance down the hill, St. Ives revealed a small cove encircled by a former fishing village turned summer tourist magnet with stone cottages sporting roofs of moss-covered indigenous slate. Streets barely wide enough for car traffic meandered past the homes, shops and pubs that clung to precipitous hillsides. Pedestrians walked single-file along skinny sidewalks I imagined had been built by Lilliputians. When an ambulance or delivery van needed to get by, people either backed into a doorway or flattened themselves against a wall, angling to avoid a scrape from side-view mirrors. Brilliantly hued flowers cascaded from window boxes on many buildings, creating a travel-poster vista of vacation paradise. Every store clerk greeted customers with cheer and smiles. And Cornish-tinged English rang out in greeting: "Here you go, me darlin'," or "How can I help, dearie?" Not a skeleton-faced Mrs. Danvers from *Rebecca* appeared among the lot. How could I possibly put myself into du Maurier's gloomy world when everyone exuded such cheery friendship?

Perhaps the notorious Jamaica Inn, setting for the eponymous movie and novel, would provide the gothic inspiration I sought. It certainly inspired du Maurier. For over 260 years this coach stop, inn and tavern welcomed travelers as well as smugglers, highwaymen and other ne'er-do-wells. Located on a lonely stretch of road through notorious Bodmin Moor, its desolate location still overlooks a windswept and treacherous landscape. Currently a modern hotel and pub, the Jamaica Inn maintains the atmosphere of du Maurier's story as well as celebrating its own sordid history. There's even a brass plaque on the floor marking where Joss Merlyn, the arch villain in the book, was murdered. Stories abound of how ships were lured onto Cornwall's brutal rocks by deviously placed beacons. Just like in the novel, the real Jamaica Inn hosted many land-based pirates and provided storage for their stolen cargos. With ghosts of murder victims reportedly roaming its halls, it's considered one of Great Britain's most haunted locations.

However, I failed to spot any restless spirits wearing tricorne hats, boots and knee breeches. Instead, on the day of our visit, I stood in the front yard, surveying the tourists with their buses and cars. The sky was clear, the sun warm and even the hostelry's roadway sign appeared cheerful, depicting a pirate and his parrot painted in Disney-like brilliant colors. The place seemed too inviting and colorful to instill in me an intimate sense of its truly horrific past.

Still seeking the mysterious darkness of Manderley, I headed to Fowey (pronounced *foy*), where du Maurier rented her cherished Menabilly for over twenty years. Once there, I discovered that the fabled home of Fowey's most famous citizen is still owned by the Rashleigh family who acquired it from King Henry VIII. It remains a private residence closed to the public, but part of the estate can be seen from the road returning to St. Ives. As we passed it, I craned my neck to see the landscape stretching out below in a long slope to a distant thick wood and the sea beyond. Sheep with black faces and puffy wool coats dotted emerald-hued fields defined by dark green hedgerows. Not even a roof-line or chimney of the historic building peeked above the foliage. My dream of finding Manderley evaporated as the idyllic pastoral scene slipped past our windows.

Looking for my portal into a murky world had turned depressing. I couldn't find a single bit of melancholia with which to commune. Perhaps a vestige of the Dark Ages could kindle the illusive doldrums. Tintagel Castle might provide stimulation for my long-sought gothic darkness. A crumbled remnant, it clings to a vertigo-inducing rocky island that caps a jutting coastal peninsula. Legends place the birth of mythic King Arthur there or claim it as the true location of Camelot. The story of Arthur involves universal and time-honored themes: from the delightfully bleak—such as murder, betrayal, tragic love triangles, forbidden romance, and black magic—to higher-minded quests, such as those for the divine, for noble warriors fighting for good, gallantry, chivalry and for Christian virtue. These tales gave content and structure to much of the world's great literature. In Arthurian legend, Cornwall had nurtured a far more monumental literary saga than du Maurier's books. Tintagel provided the symbolic cradle for generations of writers, artists, and even a few musicians.

Searching the ruins for that creative spark, however, requires an intrepid spirit along with mountain goat DNA. A treacherous footpath runs along the flank of a shale-strewn hill where Tintagel's ruins stand, taking visitors to a flat grassy area at the end of the peninsula and rock walls that once formed an initial barrier gate. A dazzling vista lies below with a cove only large enough for a few rowboats. On the sparkling clear day that I visited, the view of this rugged Cornish coast reached to the northern horizon. In order to trek Tintagel's island though, hikers must descend shale stairs at a terrifying angle toward a footbridge hundreds of feet below. For me, acrophobia made it unthinkable to even attempt the first step. Instead, left behind, I watched as others got themselves down the stairs then ascended the hundred-plus steps on the other side of the bridge and on to explore the island's ruins. Perhaps I would at last find the melancholy I had been seeking.

But while gazing at brilliant green grass contrasting with outlines of wet rocks, the diamond sparkles of sunlight on the ocean and the sheer inaccessibility of the place, light and beauty had chased away the funereal in my spirit. I remembered, too, how as an excessively sentimental teenager, the story and music of King Arthur, as told on Broadway and in celluloid, had seized my over-active imagination. Suddenly I recalled magical set designs in vivid Technicolor and my adolescent yearning for romance and drama. Once more my memory swelled with Richard Burton singing,

*Don't let it be forgot that once there was a spot*
*For one brief shining moment that was known as Camelot.*

Then it struck me; I had found what I really sought. I replaced Manderley with Camelot.

Author's father, Joseph Francis Pramik

# BLACK TO GRAY AND BACK

*MJ Pramik*

The scent of machine oil caught at the back of my throat. Late afternoon light hung throughout the vacant Geevor Mine's tin washing room. A solitary fly buzzed in the yawning October air. The sharp smell of spent black grease brought up a vision of my father in our frigid basement unraveling his body from lubricant-immersed coveralls. Bent over and weary, muscles knotted from ten to twelve hours in the mine, he'd peel off the black- and gray-striped work clothes and toss them directly into the Double Dexter washing machine. His body sweat mixed with machine oil. The intermingling of these two smells identified my father during my early years in rural Ohio.

My thoughts raced in synch with the rumbling and rocking of the second-class rail car from London thumping me to St. Ives and the Geevor Tin Mine in Cornwall—that western finger of England poking into the Atlantic. Riotous British graffiti danced on passing empty coal cars. The syncopated clatter of the train and the vacant railcars sparked memories from the past of my coalminer father down in the tunnels below the earth's surface. The Cornwall guidebook noted that visitors could go underground into the Geevor Mine. This cinched it: I had always wanted to know how and what my father felt in the bowels of the earth. He was a quiet man, not given to embellishments, favoring one-or two-word answers. I wanted to feel what he felt in the blackness.

The Wheal Mexico, Geevor Mine's main dig, is estimated to be 250 years old. It operated as a tin-producing site until 1990, when the element's price crashed, rendering the operation unprofitable. At that time, the mine linked eighty-five miles of twisting tunnels, requiring on average a million gallons of water siphoned out daily. Black tin still rests under the Geevor surface, too costly to remove. The Geevor Mine now functions as a tourist venue. The land encircling the refurbished mine buildings stands bare, pocked with random chaparral ending at the Atlantic bluffs.

Descending into today's Geevor mineshaft required little courage on my part. The smooth, well-designed path alleviated any chance of my slipping or falling into a shaft. It almost seemed like a visit to Disneyland, with the Atlantic Ocean crashing off the cliffs.

I donned a burgundy laboratory coat and yellow hardhat to tour the Wheal Mexico. In the fully operating mine, the Geevor worker would descend via sets of long wooden ladders down 350 to 500 feet below the surface. However, I stepped through a passageway that dropped only ninety feet underground. Once inside the two-foot wide shaft, my eyes quickly adjusted to minimal light. My body crouched only slightly in the short tunnel. The average height of the Cornish miner was recorded at five feet, two inches. My height.

Mine owners and the miners themselves considered it unlucky for women to enter the shafts. Females worked above ground. Known as Bal Maidens or Bal Maids, they smashed rock chunks into fragments and sorted ore from rocks by hand. Boys as young as five labored in the mine. Ten year olds loaded rocks into kibbles or large buckets, while fourteen year olds, considered grown men, could detonate gunpowder. My father started his coal mining life at age fourteen, leaving off high school as commanded by his strict father. This memory hit me full force in the dim light, and saddened me as it always did. My father had placed first in a statewide test. Not attending high school created a huge hole in his life.

In the Geevor shaft, I ran my hand across the cold, damp wall. *I must remember to thoroughly scrub my hands because of the arsenic lacing the rockshaft,* I reminded myself. Miners ate below during their workday rather than climb hundreds of feet up wooden ladders to the surface. Squatting in a tiny cutout room, the men would grasp their meat pie—called a pasty—by the crust's thickened end. They would discard this edge to avoid arsenic poisoning.

Tin mining required the men to work looking upward to hammer out the ore. They'd slither sideways through narrow shafts. Average life expectancy of a Cornish miner during the 1800s was twenty-four years. Accidents were frequent and many. In *Hazards & Heroes in Cornish Mines,* by Allen Buckley, I'd read of teenager Jack Jarvis who stepped onto loose rock and plummeted seven meters into a stope (ore dig out). According to Buckley, "Jack lay there, fully conscious, but with a large piece of rock embedded in his skull and his legs and lower body buried by the rocks which had fallen with him." After extensive effort, fellow miners hauled him out, and he returned to the mine six months later with a dent in his head that lasted his lifetime. Cornwall miners, young and old, faced death by gassing with carbon monoxide, explosions from gunpowder and later dynamite, or sudden flooding of the entire shaft as storms pounded the sea against the tunneled cliffs.

Standing hunched in the black shaft lit by tiny bulbs, I thought of Jack Jarvis and tasted the dust hanging in the damp. Cornish men had eaten this dust daily. So had Ohio miners. In March 1940, dust from an extreme explosion of methane gas devastated the Willow Grove Mine, five miles from my rural Ohio home. Of 180 workers in the mine at that time, seventy-three died. Madeline Kanopsic, our long-time next-door neighbor, lost her husband Albert at age thirty-three that day. Madeline, pregnant with their first child, could never recall how she survived the ensuing months.

The Willow Grove Mine, owned by Hanna Coal Company, my father's employer, boasted this "non-gaseous" mine to be state of the art. Five years earlier, First Lady Eleanor Roosevelt had toured its underground two miles of shafts. After the explosion of black powder and invisible methane gas, with a force that tore hinges off steel doors and split girders as if matchsticks, all mines were deemed gaseous. But seventy-three men lost their lives before mine owners admitted the constant danger.

Like their Cornish counterparts in tin mine disasters, mine superintendent John Richards and outside tipple foreman Howard Sanders raced into the Willow Grove Mine to rescue their coworkers. Several men dragged out comatose miners and revived them. However, Richards and Sanders searched further into the tunnels. They then collapsed, dying from afterdamp—unseen carbon monoxide gas. Twenty-three men survived the Willow Grove blast by losing consciousness on their three-mile journey to the mine's entrance. Their faces lay on the ground near the "good air."

Emerging from the Geevor shaft, I inhaled swiftly and deeply, unaware I'd held my breath for quite a while inside. I gasped, too, for the generations of Cornish men and boys who readied themselves each day for death—much like the Polish and Slavic miners did in eastern Ohio.

As writer Daphne du Maurier observed in *Vanishing Cornwall*, "Superstition flows in the blood of all three peoples"—though she meant the Cornish, Bretons and Irish, she well could have included the Polish-Americans I know. Du Maurier continued, "Rocks and stones, hills and valleys, bear the imprint of men who long ago buried their dead beneath great chambered tombs and worshipped the earth goddess."

My father, working in eastern Ohio's black tunnels as did his fore-bears in southern Poland's underground labyrinths, wore scapular medals—amulets of sorts—to the Black Madonna, the Lady of Czestochowa and other saints for protection from cave-ins, injury and death. Methodism guided Cornish miners, while Catholicism brought the balm of community to my hometown.

Du Maurier might well have described my father when she wrote, "There is in the Cornish character, smoldering beneath the surface, ever ready to ignite, a fiery independence, a stubborn pride." An early member of the United Mine Workers of America, my father was as stubborn as any Cornishman, laboring a long shift underground only to come home to hoe his quarter-acre garden in the summer dusk; or as he walked the picket line when forced to strike against unsafe and unfair labor practices.

He made his livelihood and cared for his five children by plunging into the underground daily. He left home at eleven o'clock at night on the midnight shift, his biorhythms askew and inverted. The Cornish miners felt the same as they left the sunshine to their families above ground. In his waning years, my father recalled with crystal clarity his days down in the bowels of the earth. "It was cool and quiet. You could do your work in silence. You'd hear only the hammer hitting the coal and rocks."

Yet for him, like for all miners, the specter of death was always present. His Polish ancestors never wished for a quick death. They would pray: "From pestilence, famine, fire, war and sudden, unexpected death, preserve us, O Lord." The worst to happen was to meet death unprepared —away from home, lacking funds for a proper burial or in a state of sin.

As I climbed out of the Geevor mine, I thought of the Bible that served both the Cornish miners and my father's people. The passage that said, "*from dust we came and to dust we shall return.*" Coal dust. Tin

135

dust. Black or gray, much the same. My mouth felt stuffed with cotton balls.

The Atlantic heaved and crashed against the boulders below. Sea air and sunshine brightened the late afternoon. I somewhat expected men and boys to pour out of the shafts and machine rooms, headed home to their families and a sturdy supper.

My first venture into Cornwall had brought to the surface neglected memories long submerged. The whiff of machine oil, a creak of a crank, dimness at ninety feet underground took me to my father's world. His work in the mines sustained him and his family.

My father has now been permanently underground for seven years. What would he think about today's move away from coal, about the push to leave all fossil fuels underground? Today I understand that mining— ripping open the earth's innards to release carbon, fuel homes, adjust economies, and enrich the uber-wealthy—assures and guarantees the destruction of the planet.

Verdant fields encircling the Geevor site added to the poignancy of the moment. I felt my father standing beside me, surveying the landscape with his approving crooked smile.

Remains of tin mines punctuate the Cornish countryside

# Bringing It Back Home

*Kitty Hughes*

The devil himself would never cross the River Tamar into Cornwall for fear of ending up as a pasty filling—so goes a Cornish tale. This visitor advisory resonates with me. I grew up in the Ozarks where a version of an old fiddle tune called "The Arkansas Traveler" recounts how an uncouth backwoodsman played devilish tricks on an unwary city slicker.

I asked a taxi driver in Penzance if visitors from elsewhere had any favorite ethnic slurs for the natives of this far-flung piece of England. He threw me a sarcastic laugh, adding, "No, all they have to say is, 'They are Cornish.'"

Then I have to laugh. In California, where I live now, "Arkie" is an epithet that says it all. Sometimes I may as well have come from Mars, as when someone says, "I never met anyone from there before!"

The Romans pretty much left Cornwall alone when they colonized Brittania in the first to fifth centuries CE; the territory was too wild and the inhabitants too unruly, best left out of the picture. The name of the Celtic tribe, the Dumnonii, who controlled the area, may have meant "deep valley dwellers," possibly derived from the name of the goddess of the deep. "Dumnonii" may also mean "masters," from the Latin "*dominus*," reflecting their savage control.

For centuries, northern and eastern England looked upon Cornwall as foreign territory with scary inhabitants. The ocean, with its rugged coastline punctuated by treacherous shoreline caves, as well as the unfamiliar mountainous terrain and trackless moors, helped isolate it—and provided its allure.

Not unlike Cornwall, the Ozarks are known as a barbarous outpost of the American South. The woodsy hills and plateaus, with hidden hollows, caverns and raging creeks, isolated the original settlers there, who lived for over a century with little contact with the outside world. This gave rise to the cultural stereotype known as "the hillbilly," the half-civilized mountain man reclining on a front porch rocker, smoking a corncob pipe, with a rifle slung across his lap.

When I visited the town of Fowey in Cornwall, other resemblances between Cornwall and the Ozarks bombarded me. Fowey is a small port town of some few thousand residents built on the hills at the foot of the River Fowey. I was comfortable in its small scale and relaxed atmosphere, even if it was overrun with tourists. Taking a rest from exploring the winding streets and harbor views, I bought a book at the nearby bookstore and sat down in the quiet courtyard of the medieval church of St. Finbarrus to look through it.

The book featured photographs of Cornish tin miners taken in the mines in the 1890s. In the images, the miners, both adults and young boys, never pose or smile for the photographer. They stare at us across time, with grim expressions and a quiet dignity, never lifting their hands from their work.

My mind leapt to Dorothea Lange's photographs of the Okies and Arkies, poor dirt farmers, driven out by the Dust Bowl. I also saw the face of the Appalachian miner's wife, pensively coming to terms with her dim future, with her hand resting on her cheek. All these faces without self-pity show the longing for another life and the will to somehow persevere.

There is a saying in Cornwall that "you will always find a Cornishman at the bottom of a pit." In America, other Celts showed up to do the job as well, picking and blasting away the rocks deep in the earth. My own ancestors were Welsh coal miners in Pennsylvania. My grandfather Hughes, a Vaudeville actor in the early 1900s, joined the movement to abolish the practice of using child labor in the mines. On the Chautauqua Circuit, he travelled around the country, performing a heart-rending monologue of a Welsh miner mourning the loss of his son to raise public awareness of this social ill.

Cornish miners were stuck in the dark tunnels, while Ozark farmers labored on rocky, unproductive soils, neither group able to improve their poor living conditions. Not surprisingly, there is a history of underground economies as well: Cornwall had its rum runners and smugglers, the Ozarks, its moonshine stills and vigilante justice.

And just as the mining tunnels of Cornwall gave birth to the piskies and giants that plagued the hapless miners, the caverns and rock ledges of the Ozarks gave birth to creatures like the "Gowrow," a monstrous lizard that laid eggs the size of beer kegs and ate the farmers' cattle. If the Cornish love their Beast of Bodmin, a giant feral cat that stalks the moors, the Ozarkians venerate their razorback, a ferocious hog with an uber-sawtoothed back turned football icon.

Possessed by this rich vein of cultural comparisons, I began to wonder more about the worldviews shared by folk historically separated from the cultural mainstream. I asked Elaine Clark, a volunteer greeter at the Fowey Museum in Cornwall, about the Cornish temperament. She stood a little straighter when she confided in me: "The people here are open to newcomers, barring those who want to take over. The worst thing is for someone to look down on you and treat you as if you are stupid because of your southern accent."

"Southern accent," she said. I knew what she meant. A final piece of the puzzle fell into place for me. In the Ozarks, the locals are known to be friendly but become defensive when they hear their accent or way of life derided. And when strangers arrive, they better watch what they say.

Elaine felt familiar to me. She was chatty, making time for the kind of leisurely talk that people in the South are known for. The similarities were actually part of a continuum. I was enjoying the legacy of the Celtic oral traditions that passed through my family's Welsh side for generations and took root in the Ozarks.

So, culturally, Elaine and I were related. The Scotch-Irish, as well as migrants from Wales and Southeast England, made their way west from Appalachia, where they first settled. They went looking for new land in the Ozark Plateau by the early 1840s. Even today you can hear their distinctive stamp on the folk music, folklore and local expressions, brought across the Atlantic Ocean and preserved back in the hills. I had done my share of touring around in Cornwall, but it was only when I stopped to talk with people that I found this deeper connection.

In the South, conversation is an entertainment and a way of passing the time, as I sense it is for the Cornish. On the way to Tintagel from St. Ives, our bus driver regaled us with countless stories and offered his opinions on Prince Charles, the British government, John Wesley, Methodism, and the class structure of St. Ives. He relished all the questions we asked him and, like the southerners I know, would go to great lengths to keep the conversation going. Sometimes he did not give us a straight answer—a good southern strategy for keeping the listener engaged and curious.

Whenever I call my friends and relatives back home, I joke that I can never get off the phone. Just when I'm about to hang up, I hear the familiar refrain, "Oh, there is one other thing I forgot to ask you."

As I talked with Elaine, another similarity grabbed me—the hold of traditions and heritage on the local psyche. Elaine's family has lived in

Cornwall for over 500 years, as she told me with pride. The one-room museum where we stood is housed in one of the oldest buildings in Fowey, dating back to the fifteenth century. The artifacts make enduring connections to Elaine's family's past: glassed-in exhibits of clay pipes rescued from shipwrecks, ship-building tools, swords from ancient wars, and recent World War II memorabilia.

The Fowey town seal, dated 1688, is painted on a slab of wood and hangs on the far wall, carefully preserved away from the light, its antique veneer shimmering. I quickly calculated that Elaine's ancestors were living in the town by then and probably knew this building. As an American, it is difficult for me to comprehend a family history as deep and imbedded in place as Elaine's. Yet the precious quality of things from the past was so alike.

In the Ozarks, small museums and families prize their collections of Native American arrowheads found along creek beds; spinning wheels; farming equipment and quilts from pioneering days; Civil War swords; and decommissioned tractors. As at the Fowey Museum, these are humble artifacts, nothing grand like the collections of the big well endowed museums. And they are not simply objects arranged for viewing, but living evidence of a personal connection to place.

One glass case in the Fowey Museum displays many pairs of shoes that were hidden in the walls centuries ago to ward off evil spirits that might bring bad luck. The faded shoes are lined up by size, from children's slippers to adult button-ups. By the number of pairs on display, it is not hard to imagine that the practice of sequestering shoes was fairly widespread.

The Ozarks were rife with similar practices in the nineteenth and early twentieth centuries. Many of these practices undoubtedly traveled there with the Celts who settled in the mountain hollows. At table it was bad form to take a saltshaker from another person's hand, since this might bring evil fortune to both parties; you were to wait until your neighbor set the saltshaker down on the table and withdrew his hand, then you were free to pick it up.

It is hard for us today to imagine a world so animated by spirits, although some say the Celt has always been plagued by an overactive imagination and dark, brooding thoughts. William Butler Yeats, the Irish poet, saw another side, cultivating the notion of the noble savage attuned to natural beauty. I like to think that some of this savage nature has still survived in us moderns.

The bus I took to Tintagel careened around the twisting roads, through green hills like mounded pillows, past ancient stones stacked into walls and monuments. Between the hills, glimpses of a swath of slate-blue sea appeared. Our bus driver proudly pointed out the features of the land, even as he decried the persistence of poverty and dependence on tourism to boost the economy.

I suddenly missed the sheltering hills, the craggy bluffs and the creeks that twist through the Ozarks. Some of the poorest old-timers surviving on meager incomes there, despite the new Wal-Mart economy, call it "God's country" and would never live anywhere else.

Surfing at St. Ives

# LIFE'S A BEACH
# ON THE CORNISH COAST

*Thomas Harrell*

"This was rated the third best beach in the world."

I followed the sweep of the cabdriver's hand, startled, as he gestured to the sand below the parking lot where we stood. Wait a minute: Had we taken a terribly wrong turn and landed in Brazil instead of on Cornwall's famously stormy Atlantic coast? Did he not realize I was from California, that these were fighting words? I mean, did the Beach Boys sing about the bikinis of Cornwall?

After a journey of six thousand miles on two airplanes and two trains, I was prepared to accept, indeed celebrate, the romance of Cornwall: the pirates, piskies, smugglers, and even the Knights of the Round Table. But the best beaches too? It seemed a tad greedy.

I silently conceded the beach below us seemed charming. Families of locals and tourists—the latter pasty-white or beet-red—took advantage of the unseasonable sunshine to relax or play in sand the color of fresh butter. A sweeping crescent bay stretched to the horizon, and an island with a lighthouse added mystery and atmosphere, like some Victorian beauty mark on the blue-gray sea.

When I arrived in St. Ives I knew little except that it was on the coast, in Cornwall, and fancied itself an arts center. I had deliberately avoided reading much about the town, opting for surprise over familiarity. After a week in St. Ives, I think the greatest surprise was just how familiar the town felt to a tourist from California.

I had not planned, or packed, for a beach vacation. You do not go to England for the beaches. And Cornwall? Stuck between the Atlantic Ocean and the English Channel, it hardly suggests board shorts and suntan lotion. And though I had packed plenty of warm socks and two raincoats—but nothing resembling a swimsuit—for my writing adventure, the cabbie's casual remark was like a glove to the face: a challenge no gentleman from California could refuse. Honor demanded an investigation.

St. Ives boasts an enviable location on the western tip of St. Ives Bay, with a view east across the bay that requires never less than ten minutes of admiration. It juts into the ocean and enjoys water on three sides. But until Victorian times the view of the water was far less important than what lay beneath the water: the tens of millions of pilchards (sardines) caught every year by St. Ives fishermen for export the world over. Only with the completion in 1877 of the picturesque trunk train line from St. Erth to St. Ives, connecting St. Ives to London, did the town's transition from fishing to art and tourism begin in earnest.

Still, a "Cornish Riviera"? The talk of warm currents and a Mediterranean climate had seemed—if you'll excuse the pun—like so much hot air ... until I'd alighted from the St. Erth trunk line. The sun blazed. I shaded my eyes as I searched for a cab. I found Michael Pryce, a long-time St. Ives cabbie, waiting in the small parking lot. Michael was the first reminder of home. With his long hair, weathered tan, and obvious pride in his locale, he could have stepped from any San Francisco street corner. Indeed, he looked like a veteran of the Summer of Love, with a Cornish accent.

The day, too, conspired to remind me of home. As we would be reminded many times that week, it was "unseasonably" warm in St. Ives, just as California had been "unseasonably" dry for four years. Okay, St. Ives sun and sand. And blue water. But I wasn't yet convinced I had landed on a Riviera.

I have been to some of the world's most famous beaches, from Bondi in Australia to Clifton by Capetown, from surfing beaches in Oahu to walking beaches along Big Sur. At each there is an unmistakable sense of place. To my mind, you can't simply mix and match water, sand, rock, waves, add palm trees and surfer dudes, and dazzle with the alchemy of a great beach.

As I see it, a great beach begins in the toes and ends in the eyes, and seduces all the senses in between. This, then, was my mission: Open myself to seduction and hope for love. Someone had to do it!

St. Ives has four main beaches. Being methodical, or perhaps simply lazy, I started close to our accommodations at Tregenna Castle. A ten-minute walk downhill, along typically British pedestrian paths, through lush trees and flowering plants, brought me to a bluff overlooking Porthminster Beach. "Porth" is a common prefix for beaches throughout Cornwall and means "saint" in Cornish, a reference to the arrival of St. Ia from Ireland in the fifth century.

I wondered if St. Ia landed at Porthminster. I hoped so; I liked Porthminster immediately. As you narrow your eyes and peer through the red and pink foliage, you see green, then sand, and then blue water. Robinson Crusoe would feel at home.

As you walk closer to the beach, you begin to see the sweep of St. Ives Bay and the iconic homes and harbor of St. Ives. Robinson Crusoe may fade from the imagination, but the granite and tile homes anchor you immediately in Cornwall.

Surely the most famous landmark in St. Ives Bay, and a beacon from Porthminster, is the lighthouse. It stands near the mouth of the bay, shrouded at times in the haze. The air of mystery is delightfully British. The lighthouse is said to have inspired Virginia Woolf's *To the Lighthouse*. I knew then, without a doubt, I was not in Brazil, or Thailand, despite the palm trees. I was in Cornwall.

On my last day in St. Ives, we were again favored with brilliant sunshine. It truly felt like California. Porthminster was filled with families. Gulls fought for scraps. Dogs slept in the shade. I lunched at the Porthminster Cafe on the beach, and found myself again feeling at home. The menu could have graced any California restaurant; even the fish and chips were deconstructed. Floor-to-ceiling windows captured the scene. Did I linger? Of course I did.

At the other end of town, literally and figuratively, is Porthmeor Beach. It sits below the Tate Modern St. Ives and a host of art galleries, but it is not a watercolor beach. It is the surfing beach, the beach for waves and currents and risk, a challenging beach.

I sat on one of the benches that line the bluff above Porthmeor and watched the surfers. I was reminded of northern California, even Ocean Beach on the Pacific in San Francisco. Surfers were clad head to toe in wetsuits like upright seals. But I could see St. Ives to my right, and the Tate behind me. The setting was incongruous and captivating at the same time. The sun set as I stood. Surfers from Hawaii or South Africa might scoff at the small beach and tame waves (just wait for winter), but for a corner of Britain known more to the world for pirates and pilchards than taming waves, I was impressed.

The walk back toward Tregenna Castle from Porthmeor takes you near Porthgwidden Beach. Porthgwidden seemed to me a quintessential British experience: Small—perhaps more a cove than a beach—and off the beaten path, it requires an effort to discover its charms. Surprisingly, little Porthgwidden reminded me of far grander European beaches on the French and Italian Rivieras. Protected by headlands on each side from the wind and surf, it is a peaceful respite from crowded St. Ives. And the row of beach pavilions at Porthgwidden could have been lifted from a resort a thousand miles south. It was a beach that demanded a good book and a nap.

But I think my favorite beach in St. Ives was the least familiar, and at times not even a beach. It was Harbour Beach, and as the name implies, it is at the harbor. St. Ives has not turned its back on its history. The harbor at St. Ives is a working harbor. Fishing boats still pursue the pilchards. At low tide the boats wallow on their sides in the wet, seaweedy sand, the mooring lines lying by the dozens in parallel. When the water is out, the sand is in, and strange as it may seem, this patch of sand, between the harbor on one side and the main tourist drag on the other, is remarkably, almost unbelievably, peaceful.

I loved the contrast of the bustle behind; the ice cream shops and bistros and galleries; the children and the gulls, both crying over spilled food; and the ancient, methodical workings of the harbor, timeless like the tides. One side is for the ears, the other the eyes.

And in between is a sliver of sand, a peekaboo beach, to bridge the two worlds. Twice I bought fish and chips, the old-fashioned deep-fried kind made from the local catch, and sat watching the tide rise to hide the beach, and recede to make room for towels and pale bodies. It was the old St. Ives and the new.

I returned to California a touch less parochial. Were the beaches in St. Ives among the best in the world? I suppose the jury, like the tide, is still out. Beaches are like vacations: it all depends. The beaches of St. Ives are not the biggest, or the whitest, or the most crowded (thankfully). But on a tiny spit of land you can travel from the South Pacific to northern California with a detour through Italy on your way to a meal of fried fish fresh off the boat.

And isn't a great vacation a mix of the familiar and the novel? I think so. I bought a swimsuit in London, of all places, on my way home. Next time, no matter how far I travel, I will be prepared.

St. Ives Bookseller

# IN SEARCH OF FELICITY

*Antoinette Constable*

I had come to Cornwall after a lengthy intercontinental tour that involved visits to rarely seen relatives in a number of countries. Although I was tired, I was also excited and determined to meet a local writer of detective stories, one Debbie Fowler, whose knowledge of plot, human drama and resolution are the foundation of the craft. I wanted to learn from her the secret of plotting. In exchange I would offer her a suggestion—I'd heard she was shy—on signing her books without embarrassment. We would both be happy. I was filled with glowing anticipation. Clear and easy— isn't happiness simple to reach?

Thanks to Debbie Fowler, Felicity Paradise, Cornwall transplant and accidental sleuth, had taken me into several crime novels such as *Smoke Damage, Letting Go, In a Small Town* and so on. In each, I enjoyed the British contemporary language; a Cornish setting of beaches, rocks, fog, and wind; and tea always offered in a cheerful kitchen, near an ever-present AGA stove. I also enjoyed touches of humor and lively characters I might easily have met along the boardwalk, in restaurants or supermarkets in any Cornish town.

I was excited and wanted to meet her to ask whether she started her novels with characters whom she will place in danger, or whether she first conceives of a tremendous problem to be handled by people with an assortment of motives. How did she manage to ratchet up each crisis, keeping it believable and yet inevitable, as she created her dramas?

In addition to her crime novels, Debby Fowler has written more than six hundred stories for women's magazines and, with her husband, produced books of non-fiction on topics as varied as adoption, money management, and guide books for small businesses. Clearly, a Cornish woman eminently clever and worth meeting.

I live in sunny California, where I had recently learned that this most modest of women writers was too discreet to reveal that she was the author of the detective novels for sale in her shop. She could easily get over that obstacle, I was burning to suggest, by asking her clients whether they would like an autographed copy. She could then sign her book in front of the startled and delighted customer, or go behind a partition and return, smiling proudly with a reward for the individual already opening his or her wallet. Extravagantly pleased with my idea, I looked forward to presenting it in person, in the briefest delay, to Debby Fowler, creator of the Felicity Paradise mystery series.

When I reached promising Cornwall, offering bays and boats, sun, saints, caves, mist and mysteries, I found St. Ives filled not so much with the passion and envy of Debbie Fowler's Felicity Paradise mysteries, but with fuchsia and enormous red and yellow begonias. I immediately inquired at Tregenna Castle about the bookstore in town where Cornish Felicity reigned, and my first disappointment stood as stiff as a plank in front of me. Of the two booksellers in town, the one I longed to visit no longer existed.

I refused to be discouraged. Like an obstreperous child, intent on a promised but suddenly withheld treat, I decided the missing bookstore was no problem, because surely there must be a way; the Internet would be my guide. My second disappointment rose from my flat magic box.

The computer offered neither street address, phone number nor email address. Now frustration was not an eleven letter word used by crossword designers or psychologists no longer experiencing that most irritating of emotions. This absence of information ran all over my skin like a burning nettle rash, impossible to ignore.

The cure, I believed, might be a visit to the remaining bookseller in town. I would throw myself at the owner's knees, in the way of ancient Greeks and Romans, and beg to be handed that indispensable salve to recover both my mental and physical equilibrium. I urgently needed to meet Felicity's creatrix.

Under an overcast sky, I ran across cobblestones in the narrow streets of St. Ives, bumping into tourists, scooting past gift stores, Cornish pasty shops and art galleries. At a hilly corner, I found the remaining white-painted shop, simply called, St. Ives Bookseller. I raised my sandaled feet over the few stone steps and almost danced into the bookstore. A customer retreated, paper bag under one arm, handbag on the other. In my eagerness, I inched as close as possible to the register, my heart almost exploding with a hope I tried to disguise. I nonchalantly asked the clerk whether she sold Felicity Paradise books.

"Oh," she said, turning her lovely young face toward me," Sorry, Love, I just sold the last copy of the most recent novel."

"I so much wanted to read it! But what I want even more is to contact Debbie Fowler. Could you help me find her?"

"Mmmm. That's not going to be easy," she answered, shaking her head.

I stood, dumbstruck, my legs not salt, but granite pillars, my heart stumping drunkenly in my chest. I had wanted so much to meet her, to talk with her, to ask for her literary suggestions before offering my own.

In the end, the clerk wrote down an email address for Debbie Fowler. I sent the writer an urgent message to which I never received a reply. I didn't receive an answer to my message, but a friend who'd already read two of her books gave me *In a Small Town* and *Smoke Damage* before I left Cornwall. I gave up hope of communicating with Debbie Fowler, but I somehow I managed to acquire four more Felicity Paradise mysteries, which I share with various friends. I have become a sort of private library spreading the word of Debbie Fowler and, I might add, every chance I get, a little felicity.

St. Ives Arts Club

# St. Ives Journals

*Sandra Bracken*

It's been a challenge, scouring my journals for this timeline: getting lost in the past, lingering there. It's also somewhat sad to have to leave out so much of this history. The journal entries I chose are only a few of hundreds. I condensed them severely. It all goes back to that week in 1983. Despite my instinct to be a loner—a spectator, not a participant— I was surprisingly, but quite agreeably, pulled into the lives of four people.

### 10 July, 1983, St. Ives

Walking slowly up the worn steps to the St. Ives School of Painting, I was nervous. I'd signed up for an art class in another country. Would I fit in? I wasn't a painter. My approach to art was more conceptual. I intended to draw. Would they think I was a rebellious, arrogant American? Reaching the last step, curiosity had changed to anxiety as I pushed open the heavy blue door.

Once again I was on my own, leaving my family briefly to travel, to focus on art. From previous trips I'd learned I liked the anonymity of traveling alone: I liked being the fly on the wall, the observer. I liked the freedom of being able to change direction as the mood suited me. No wonder I was uneasy knowing I had committed to being in one place for one week. My comfortable pattern, one that worked well for me, was about to change.

## Journal Entries: 10 and 14 July, 1983, St. Ives

This was my second trip to the UK. Four years out of grad school, I had a studio for constructing sculpture, taught drawing and was curious to see the wider world of art and artists.

*In hand my receipt and letter of acceptance signed by Roy Ray, director of the school. Surprise ... he was the tutor! Friendly, approachable, everything was in order, he said. Warm welcome. He reminded me of a country western singer, black jeans, a flannel shirt, boots, forty something, dapper with mustache, goatee and graying hair. Of course I was allowed to draw; it was my week. Did he notice my relief?*

*Abruptly, mid-morning, everyone stopped working! Tea time! What? Kettle was on, cups lined up, a plate of biscuits and a tin can for 10p coins. Unheard of in my art school. But how civilized.*

*Margaret—soft voice, inquisitive eyes—introduced herself. A painter. We had lots in common: two older women, with children, who went back to school for art degrees. Her reassuring gentleness put me more at ease.*

*Somewhat amazed at how well first day went.*

## Journal Entry: 14 July, 1983

Sadly, the last day of class. Beryl, Roy's wife, prepared "the starving artists' lunch"—paté, cheese, bread, wine. In addition to running a B&B, she modeled occasionally for Life Class. Intrepid woman.

*An air of celebration reigned at The Tinners Arms in Zennor that night. I wasn't used to such effortless humor, continual laughter and heartfelt camaraderie. How long had I known Roy, Beryl, Margaret and Jim, her husband? Only a week? It felt like a wonderful forever: thoughtful conversations, walks by the sea, sharing meals or a pint in The Sloop ... feelings of belonging. I was invited into their lives—me, the solitary traveler. We shed many tears as we hugged goodbye. I felt a sense of loss in the sadness, though promises were made to write, to visit.*

*I wanted to keep those promises, but I knew how those things go.*
*When traveling, I'm suspended in time; I experience a sense of freedom.*
*I had no expectation those feelings, relationships would continue.*
*Maybe I'd send a brief note of thanks, and then we'd drift back into*
*our own worlds.*

### Journal Entry: 26 November, 1985, Maryland

Roy and Beryl were in New York on art-related business. We'd kept in touch, and they knew that whenever visiting "the colonies" they were welcome to stay with us. I wanted them to meet my husband, Pete, and our children.

*Didn't believe it would happen ... Roy and Beryl here! Met their*
*train in Baltimore. Exciting reunion. Next stop, a college basketball game*
*thrust them straightaway into our lively family. Thanksgiving too.*

*A natural raconteur, Roy described in effusive detail waking to the*
*aroma of bacon and pancakes, hearing strains of "stained glass bluegrass"*
*on the radio and the view through trees of Magothy River. How fine to see*
*our life through his eyes.*

*Sightseeing in Annapolis, four of us wandered around, a back and*
*forth easy conversation going, as if two couples who'd known each other a*
*long time. Pete just met them!*

### Journal Entry: 10 December, 1985, Maryland

Margaret was the first to write and wrote often.

*Another letter from Margaret—put aside till I had more time to con-*
*centrate. Her handwriting's impossibly tiny, often needing a magnifying*
*glass. Glad I made a glossary of her characters and specific words—her*
*"the" looks like "we." Once I thought she described a "Caesarian section.*
*On more inspection, it was a "terrible accident." If the meaning was too*

*bizarre, I'd deciphered it incorrectly. Lots of laughs at mistaken interpretations. Her letters were full of lovely lengthy details about their lives and traditions. With intriguing questions for me. Didn't want to miss any of it.*

### Journal Entry: 24 September, 1986, Exeter

Pete retired and was ready to travel with me. I was eager for him to meet Margaret and Jim.

*Margaret was the tour guide; Jim always the driver. A carefully planned route covered a lot of territory in the West Country. Their enthusiasm and pleasure in sharing it with us so apparent. Inexplicably we stopped at a cottage. The thatched roof under construction! No surprise when I climbed the ladder to take a closer look. An unanticipated thatching lesson ... how lucky! Margaret knew that I used thatching materials and techniques in my sculpture. Was that stop really accidental?*

*And why my surprise at how well they got on with Pete? Did they feel they already knew him through our lengthy letters? Was it the ease of our first hours together, the shared enthusiasms? They welcomed him like an old friend.*

### Journal Entry: 25 September, 1988, St. Ives

Margaret suggested taking another class together at the school and sharing a self-catering flat. Brilliant.

*Loved the loft, my room, great views; Margaret and Jim were on the ground floor. We fell into an easy routine. At school, none of my anxiety of five years ago. Could hear the waves breaking on Porthmeor Beach below, as Roy outlined the week's schedule. "Experimental week"—printmaking, collage, visiting artists' studios—all appealed to me. Being with Margaret I saw how she was inspired by the world around her and how well she understood her vision. She seemed to absorb colors, then put them slowly, carefully onto paper or canvas. My approach more tactile, perhaps too hurried, easily spoiling a piece.*

*A surprising invitation to dinner with Roy and Beryl; another superb Beryl meal. Always impressed by her skill, wide-ranging repertoire. My favorite, her coq au vin.*

## Journal Entry: 12 October, 1988, Polruan

When Jim retired from teaching, they moved near Fowey where they had spent many holidays. Yes, a wonderful place for a get-away.

*Each day a hike along the coast. They wanted me to see Dartmoor too. Under an ever changing sky—sun, then shadow, cooling mists, chilling rain—tall, lanky Jim led. I tried to keep up, scrambling over stony outcroppings, steering clear of soggy, boggy areas. Was stunned by the quiet beauty of Wistmans' Woods, a miniature woodland of ancient elfin-like oaks enrobed in moss. A fairyland. I understood why it was special to them.*

*Gregarious Jim, ever the clever, animated helpmate, often treated me to spontaneous outbursts of singing—his is a beautiful tenor voice.*

*Margaret and I share a passion for gardens. They took me to Lanhydrock and Cothele. But my best project inspiration came from their home garden—a tranquil stream built into their hilly side yard.*

## Journal Entry: 24 February, 2006, Scottsdale, AZ

Pete and I, having never traveled with another couple, were surprised how much we enjoyed traveling with Roy and Beryl. After Italy and Ireland, there was the road trip from Seattle to San Francisco; now, Denver to Phoenix.

*Driving from Maryland, we met Roy and Beryl at the Denver airport. Surreal to see them walk out the exit door waving to us. Next day first stop, Vail, for their morning coffee … café Americano. Thirteen days*

*south to Ouray, Durango, Santa Fe, Grand Canyon, Sedona, Phoenix.*
*Roy, an impressive videographer, pointed his camera toward the scenery*
*most times; topography of the American west—colors, shapes and textures*
*—informed his art. Occasionally he turned the camera to the back seat,*
*always when Beryl's and my eyes were closed, mouths open! Not a pretty*
*picture. Little good it did to complain … it happened over and over*
*again. Also laughable our ups and downs with motels … the ramshackle*
*one in Sedona, the posh one in Scottsdale. But no one complained. We*
*accepted the serendipity that reflected our casual timetable. Roy, a*
*professional artist with an impressive resumé, also plays guitar rather well.*
*So Pete brought his guitar along. We were treated to some special*
*impromptu performances. Valentine's Day, Roy sang and played an*
*original piece … their sweet tradition included us.*

*Thank goodness Beryl was the go-to person for food ideas. A well-*
*practiced shopper, fast and thorough, she'd be in and out of the market,*
*have a meal going in no time, while I still pondered the possibilities. I'd*
*be a disaster at running a B&B. I admired her organization, too, in the*
*way she packed only one carry-on for three weeks. I took notes. Another*
*envy: She's always stylish, at home or traveling—a coordinated wardrobe,*
*subdued colors with jewelry to match.*

**Journal Entry: 24 June, 2006, Exeter**
Our family was traveling in the UK. All thirteen of us were invited to
Margaret and Jim's home.

*Stargazey Pie—fish heads poking through the crust looking upward—*
*was the centerpiece of the groaning board in Margaret and Jim's tiny*
*dining-sitting room. She prepared it especially for us! Imagine a clown car*
*as thirteen large "clowns" (one was six foot seven) tried to squeeze into it.*

*How incredibly thoughtful—or rash—of them to invite us all!*
*Unforgettable afternoon for my grandchildren because it was obvious that*
*Margaret had shared something unique … that we would never forget.*

**Journal Entry: 27 September, 2014, St. Ives**
This time we went from London to Exeter, then on to St. Ives where
Pete stayed with Roy and Beryl, while I attended a writing workshop.

*A two-day, too short visit with Margaret and Jim before taking the*
*train to St. Ives. The view of Carbis Bay from the branch line as*
*breathtaking as the first time. Beryl met us. Enthusiastic group hug! Roy*
*was at the school. Drastic changes there—all cleaned up and*
*handicapped- accessible. Nothing like the school of yesteryear. Except,*
*the door was still blue; studio had the same floor and ceiling. But it no*
*longer leaked.*

*So happy the entire Ray family was available for dinner together.*
*We met their granddaughter. As always, much laughter, bonhomie. I've*
*missed them and our good times.*

*Other nights, we four "old things" reminisced … the "tiresome"*
*stories retold; memories; the next trip perhaps; friendship, how long we'd*
*known each other. What made it possible? Some say there's a*
*transformative atmosphere in St. Ives. Roy said synchronicity.*

*The only thing I know is thirty-two years ago, I met four people. On*
*some extraordinary level we connected, and despite living continents*
*apart, the relationships flourished. It was they who made it possible …*
*I was having none of it when I showed up at the door of the St Ives School*
*of Painting. The wonder of it still surprises me.*

A watchful gull

# At Play with the Birds and Beasts

*Ethel Mussen*

As soon as the couple left the table next to us, the fat brown gull that
had been patrolling the area flew to the surface and faced us. We were
seated at the line of tables at the edge of St. Ives just above a round cove
with a long breakwater—Smeaton's Pier at its left and sheer cliffs to the
right, famed frame for the site of Virginia Woolf's lighthouse. Maryly
was busy tasting the clotted cream on her scone; Kitty and I were stirring
our coffee concoctions. We all eyed the gull for possible intrusion, but it
remained motionless, yet watched our every bite. Clearly, we had no
crumbs to share.

People working among the array of brightly colored boats beached
in the shallow edges of the cove below us, pushing excursions, prompted
us to agree that we would like to take a real boat ride. I informed my
companions that a barker near the Ship Rescue Boathouse just up Water
Street above us was touting a noon ride to the Seal Rocks, and that if
we hurried, we might still get aboard. We finished up and left our table
and the watchful bird and headed up to the top of the boat ramp fifty
yards away.

Halfway there, we were suddenly surprised by an enormous cloud
of shrieking, swooping gulls of every color flying over us in hot pursuit of

a lone bird heading down the ramp to the beach. When we reached the top, we saw a wide-eyed tourist couple, ten feet away from a little ice cream stand, frozen in shock. The bespectacled man automatically licked his snow cone, while his diminutive blonde wife stood transfixed. Her hands still cupped the space where her own cone had once been.

"He warned us not to stand here," she told us, gesturing toward the ice cream vendor. "The bird just swooped down and grabbed it right out of my hand!"

"Share! Share!" the flock still shrieked as they mobbed the clever thief. We could not distinguish the outcome from the swirling group in the sand. We turned to the barker nearby, who laughed and declared that this happened all the time. Then he assured us there was still some room on the boat that was heading out to visit the seals, since only one other couple had boarded. If we just retraced our steps the length of Water Street and followed the strand to Smeaton's Pier, a young man would transfer us to the nearby excursion boat.

We followed his directions, passing our brown gull, still keeping watch on its territory rather than joining the rowdy throng. We descended the few wave-splashed stone steps to a small motorboat and were ferried to our captain, waiting in a moderate-sized cabin cruiser anchored in the deeper waters because the tide was out. As the captain helped us aboard, I volunteered that we were from San Francisco, and it was ironic that we should take an excursion to visit seals.

"Ah, but you have sea lions," he explained, "and these are real seals." We three nodded in relief. Well then, this would be truly different.

And truly different it proved to be. As the boat turned to the smooth open sea, we seated ourselves quietly and comfortably at first. Then Maryly moved forward near the captain. Shortly thereafter, she erupted with a shout and a gesture at the round back of a dolphin suddenly breaching ahead of us. Then another and a third, swimming alongside, leaping and diving and playing with each other and entertaining the human company. We hastened to take pictures, to "ooh" and "aah" at the acrobatics, to admire their presence, until the boat veered closer to the craggy shore, just missing the outcropping rocks. There, a few black cormorants stood guard on one red islet. And soon we approached a formation of small peaks, with two little pools of splashing waves. Here, the seals bobbed their welcoming heads as they swam within their own waters, waving noses at us to acknowledge our arrival. The captain idled the motor to extend our time together. The seals cavorted within the rocky pools, but did not venture out. For the most part we saw only bobbing heads. If they barked at us, we did not hear. The idling motor, choppy waves, and whistling wind about our heads masked any sounds.

After twenty minutes or so, we turned about and headed back to port. Almost at once, we met our waiting escort. One dolphin leaped high out of the water in greeting and raced ahead, showing us the way. Others followed along, not quite so exuberantly, but as close companions. Leap, dive, leap, dive. We in the boat stood up and waved and cheered until they stopped guiding and stayed behind as we neared St. Ives. We turned in and sidled alongside Smeaton's Pier. The tide had risen enough in our absence to allow us to come in close to the steps. We climbed these and walked toward the village. I examined the array of stacked fish and lobster pots on the edge of the quay. A young sailor walked up with me, and I asked him what fish had been caught.

"Pilchards near here" for the round pots, "and lobster more distant" for the others, he explained.

Lobster fishing means real journeys away, while the scaled fish are near at hand. I recalled being told that Cornwall ports ship kippers to the rest of the country for their English breakfast. "Pilchards are sardines," one man had said, but added "kippers" in the next breath. I remain unclear. What did remain clear was the chill wind, which left me congested and hoarse for many days, and gave Kitty a cough and something like pneumonia. But the vision of the flying dolphins surpassed the affliction.

Later that day, Maryly, who seemed not to learn from others' misfortunes, also had a cone stolen from her hand before she'd barely licked it. The vendor does a good repeat business and does not shame the gulls much, I suspect.

Aside from our breezy maritime expedition, the weekend in the village was generally balmy. The wind had been confined mostly to the water. After our sea adventure, we joined the rest of the weekend holiday crowd in the village or up at the castle. Although the local train and buses brought many visitors, other summer-clad tourists must have driven, for they strolled the lanes of St. Ives in great crowds either pushing strollers or walking a couple of dogs on leash. It seemed that the people out and about in St. Ives favored caring for two dogs instead of one: Westies, Yorkies, Maltese, Bichon Frises, and more—all with eager brown eyes and fluffy eyebrows, marched busily ahead, leading their owners. Even burly men were flanked by dogs: smooth brown boxers or hounds with round faces and sturdy, muscular legs, but all in pairs.

After that it was the dogs, rather than the gulls, seals and dolphins that captured my attention. The next day, in Fowey, I was greeted by a brace of whippets, six or seven at the least. Another day, walking down High Stannack Street from the Leach Pottery, I met a woman with two different small dogs on leash: one a Jack Russell that belonged to her daughter, and the other her own Shih Tzu, a brown-eyed mix with shaggy eyebrows and an eager greeting demeanor.

"With those eyes she should be named Buttons," I commented, thinking of fellow traveler Unity's Shih Tzu, so aptly named.

"That would be appropriate, I guess," said this Shih Tzu's owner, "but I called her Rio. Just because. It's a grand day today, and now that the holiday is over, we can go back down to the beach."

"How do the dogs and the gulls get along?" I asked, since all the dogs I'd seen so far seemed amazingly indifferent to each other, seldom even sniffing in greeting or curiosity.

"They chase each other a little, but mostly they co-exist, sharing the sand when the tide is low and enjoying the exercise. They're all part of the same community. They're native to Cornwall."

I pondered this: the connection between the tourists and the natives and their respective interactions. Daphne du Maurier wrote her story, "The Birds," from her own Cornish coast experience, most certainly inspired by the omnipresent gulls. When Alfred Hitchcock made his film of the story, he changed the venue to Bodega Bay in northern California and the birds to black starlings. In both versions, the harassing flocks were symbols of Armageddon and spelled doom. I prefer to think that all the gulls of Cornwall have eased into a far less ominous predation. Like the other natives of the county, they need their summer visitors—as we need them.

The villages are walls of shoulder-to-shoulder dwellings, ranged against the cliffs and hillsides with narrow passageways in between, barely admitting autos, but allowing room for "foreign" pedestrians to stop and shop for pasties or crafts made by the other "foreigners"—the artists who gravitated here over the years. The "summer people" cart their babies and pets through the lanes, but must pause for food and refreshment. The museums and all of the products—from ice cream and clotted cream to pottery and art glass—serve as bait and food for the economy ... for birds and beasts and men.

Later I took pictures of the black crow scouting the horizon atop the flagpole at Tregenna Castle and a photo of a placid, puffy white gull standing watch over the port from the wall at the head of the bus stop. All natives, I thought, well fed by tourists, happily surveying their territory.

Cream tea at Camelot

# Butter and Cream

*Maryly Snow*

The mounds of Cornish clotted cream were flaxen and smooth, nothing like their name "clot" seemed to suggest, their softness an embracing counterpoint to the stones of this tiny seaside village of St. Ives. The clotted cream was on my half of the waffle. Fist-sized dollops of what looked like pale whipped butter topped the kiwi slices and blueberries on a Belgian waffle. The maple syrup seemed just right, dappling the waffle tops and pooling lightly in the bellies of all the squares. Unlike me, my breakfast companion, Ethel, would eat her half of the kiwi-blueberry-maple waffle just as Waffleicious intended, as shown on their street-side sign: waffle, fruit, syrup, no clotted cream. On my half of the waffle, however, the clotted cream looked glorious. I know that anything with a rich fat content is a necessity in countries with long, damp, cold winters, as in Mongolia, from whence I had recently returned just weeks before. But here, in the sunny fall weather, sitting outside on a warm and cloudless October day along the golden sands of the St. Ives Harbor, tide fully out, mooring lines of beached boats etching the sand, it was pure indulgence.

In a roundabout way it was my recent trip to Mongolia that inspired this idea of comparing Mongolian yak butter to Cornish clotted cream.

It was probably just an elaborate excuse to re-savor Mongolia, a way to keep that deliciously wild, open, nomadic space of a place alive while I explored the west coast of England. I had forgotten that the English are known for their creams—single, double and clotted. I also had no inkling of the disdain one shire had for the other's clotted cream, until Terry, our very funny, bald, poetry-reciting bus driver explained the difference between Cornish and Devon creams. The Cornish is a pale light gold, much the same color and texture as Mongolian yak butter, while Devon's clotted cream is reputed to be whiter, purer, "anemic," according to Terry.

The Waffleicious version of Cornish clotted cream coated the insides of my mouth and tongue with its slightly sweet, nutty, clean taste, and helped soften my youthful disdain of things English. But that had been decades ago when the English countryside, although green and fertile, had seemed too tidy and tame, so neat and enclosed, altogether too cute and claustrophobic. "Don't fence me in," had been my theme song then. At thirty, I thought I had to choose between the two, the wild and expansive versus the small and cultivated—at that young age I hadn't yet learned that I didn't need to choose, that I could love both equally.

But now, I wasn't ready for England, as I was still deeply immersed in contemplating my month on the Mongol steppe, a place that touched me profoundly. Something about its expansiveness dotted just here and there with a *ger* or two, along with herds of unfenced animals, soothed me, made me feel curiously at home. But the calendar of days is relentless: Mongolia was my past, England my present, and now I found the tidy hedgerows and narrow streets delightful and charming. Ensconced in Cornwall, I could see slivers of each, England and Mongolia, gliding past one other like tectonic plates, slipping, holding, shifting, one small, the other vast, both rich in history and shared reputations for lousy food—with the exception of their dairy.

Ah, dairy! I happily recall both places, England and Mongolia, through their dairy: Mongolia's pungent fermented mare's milk occasionally relieved by the glory of yak butter, yak yogurt, and some might say, camel's milk. I had first tried Mongolian fermented mare's milk in July. "Dorjoo," I yelled over the thrum of our four-wheel drive vehicle as we zoomed past a four-legged stool topped with a glass bottle, "what was that?"

"That was a bottle of fermented mare's milk. That means that it's for sale at that *ger*," Dorjoo shouted back.

"I want to try some!"

"We'll stop at the next place."

When Dorjoo spotted another four-legged stool topped with a bottle of milk, we stopped. Our driver, Nyama (Sunday in Mongolian), ran around to open our sliding door, reached for his blue four-legged stool, placed it on the ground, then offered each of us a hand as we stepped down onto the grassy plain. The other van stopped too, and together our party of six travelers stepped out onto one of Mongolia's few paved roads, while a herd of horses crossed lazily ahead of us.

Presently, two young nomads came running to meet us, and invited us into the family *ger*, a round felt tent much like a yurt, where even I, a mere five feet tall, had to stoop to enter the doorway. Circling to our left, as Dorjoo had taught us, we were ushered to the guests' seat of honor on the west side of the *ger*. Suddenly a small bowl of fermented mare's milk was proffered. I took a sip, surprised, not entirely pleasantly, by its penetrating, almost spoiled quality. But I knew the routine: Take a sip or two, or fake it; say something nice like "yum" or "good" before handing the bowl to the next person, bowl always in your right hand, left hand almost ritualistically touching your right elbow.

Little did I know that it wasn't necessary to buy a bottle of the stuff, as every time anyone, Mongol or foreigner, enters a nomad's *ger*, a bowl of fermented mare's milk is always offered; it's the first sign of nomadic Mongol hospitality. But I soon learned that the so-so quality of the fermented mares' milk was no match for the rich smoothness of yak yogurt and yak butter, milked from the huge silky beasts.

Days later, stricken with a wobbly tummy, I declined breakfast and asked the waitress for yak yogurt, hoping for the same smooth, cool, thick yogurt I had tasted at our *ger* camp along the unpopulated side of Lake Khovsgol in the north of Mongolia. Obligingly, she brought me a large bowl of yak yogurt. It tasted clean and pure and healthy—almost virtuous. Yak butter is slightly more common than yak yogurt, but both are infrequent treasures. Yak butter is smooth and golden with a slightly crinkled top layer, with tiny globs of brighter gold, probably glistening fat rising to the surface. In Mongolia, I was saved by yak dairy.

Perhaps I'd be saved by clotted cream in Cornwall. On a bus with others I reached the slate ruins of Tintagel Castle, dramatically clinging to the rugged terrain at the ocean's edge, supposedly King Arthur's birthplace. After clambering around, I re-boarded our bus for the short trip to a neighboring hillside and Camelot for cream tea. Camelot? How could it be? Camelot is a shining ideal, the apotheosis of chivalry and custom, built around ladies-in-waiting and knights errant—but not an actual place. If the Kennedy presidency was referred to as the "new Camelot" was this "old Camelot?" As our bus turned the corner, I saw a stucco mansion, four stories tall, boxy and square with a crenelated top. It was an 1899 hotel that seemed to have borrowed the exalted name.

Still confused, I walked in, feeling pleasantly dwarfed by its strained magnificence. In the dining room, confusion compounded as I wondered whether frisky Cornish elves, known as piskies, had scurried among the tables getting everything ready for us—each place was set with two perfectly round scones on a china plate, knife and napkin in place, the tables laden with bowls of clotted cream, red jam, and pots of tea.

For a castle named Camelot, however, the cream tea did not quite live up to expectations. The scones were heavy and dry, and the jam had the consistency of a jelly. Later, I learned this was a "refined" jam, a preserve strained of seeds and lumps and strained also, sadly, of its pleasant texture and deep fruity flavor. Still, I must admit that the clotted cream disappeared in a wink of an eye. And true to our American sensibilities, we spread it on first, like butter, followed by the jam.

That evening at Tregenna Castle I plopped myself onto a comfy couch in the lobby where wi-fi was available. Sitting across from me was the same man as the night before. What prompted us to begin chatting, I don't recall, but when I told him I was writing about clotted cream he told me, with both excitement and nostalgia, that he still remembered his grandmother making clotted cream at her home in Cornwall. She used a very large, shallow pan, four inches deep, and a foot or two long. She put the pan on the stovetop, heated the cream very slowly—cream only from Jersey or Guernsey cows because their milk has the highest fat content— and skimmed off the top layer as it thickened or clotted. That top layer was concentrated fat that oozed up from the already fat-rich cream below. Additional layers would be skimmed off and piled one on top of the other. Then the whole bowl of clotted cream layers would be refrigerated or put outside on a cold night where chilling would make the layers merge together into one smooth Cornish clotted cream. It was, he assured me, delicious.

A few days later, after a stunning taxi ride down a narrow road hemmed in by hedgerows on both sides, I found myself eating clotted cream again, this time in an altogether different environment: Geevor tin mine. After touring the site (shuttered by Margaret Thatcher in 1989), wandering down the timber-inclined warren of shaking tables where tin was separated from its chaff, visiting "The Dry" where miners changed their clothes and showered before returning home, and walking through an actual mining tunnel, I retired to the cafe.

The cream tea (scones and jam) were much better than at Camelot, although the clotted cream tasted the same, just as delicious, subtle differences lost on my untrained taste buds. But for all its delectability, something seemed wrong. It took me days to figure it out. Miners didn't eat clotted cream! Sitting in the clean, warm cafe, indulging, again, in clotted cream, seemed wrong when compared with the long, dangerous days the miners endured: digging, shoveling, chipping, loading, and lugging whatever they chopped—clay, dirt, rock, tin—out of the mine. Miners couldn't afford clotted cream, let alone wheat scones, jam, maybe even tea—all too dear and too time-consuming for a tin miner and his family. The inequity made my mouth feel slightly metallic.

Days later I moved from *Lady Chatterley*, my shared stone cottage on the grounds of Tregenna Castle, down into St. Ives proper to a very small bed and breakfast I'd found through Airbnb. My reward for lugging my suitcase, carry-on, and large purse up three narrow flights of stairs was waiting for me inside. At a small table with a full view of the St. Ives Harbor were two freshly baked scones, a bowl of jam and one of clotted cream, along with a glass of white wine. I was particularly excited because this clotted cream looked exactly like Mongolian yak butter—tiny dots of darker gold along the folds and rivulets of the clotted cream. Accompanying the clotted cream was the packaging that comes with *Rodda's Classic Cornish Clotted Cream*, available in local stores in small plastic tubs. Rodda suggests butter first, then jam, then top with clotted cream. Had I finally found the traditional way to eat clotted cream? Probably not. As Laura, my Airbnb hostess explained, "Of course, the clotted cream company would advise you to use lots and lots of clotted cream!"

I thought again about how the Mongolian yak butter and yogurt had soothed my stomach. That milk was delicious, unchurned, unfermented, just the unadorned real deal. There is no salvation in Cornish clotted cream. It is just plain rich and fatty, a total indulgence, something to be deliciously slathered on scones, pancakes, ice cream, fruit, even butter. Laura directed me to butter the fresh strawberries in my bowl, add some red jam, then heap on Cornish clotted cream. Better than Mongolian yak butter, but only just slightly.

Yum!

Hiking in Cornwall

# TREADING THE EDGE

*Lynne Rutan*

It is 8:15 a.m. and we're eager to go. The woman who boards the bus before us appears to be a proper British mum straight from BBC central casting, with her sweet smile, cloud of white hair and upper-crust accent. Although she looks like she would be most comfortable reading in an overstuffed chair, our bus mate is actually a trail-hardened veteran. She is only a few miles short of her goal to hike all 630 miles of the South West Coast Path, England's longest national trail. She has accomplished the feat bit by bit, tackling a few segments every vacation for years, but "now I can only hike three days in a row because my legs stiffen up."

"I'm seventy," she says, adjusting her daypack. "I must keep moving to finish the entire path before I'm finished."

Having hiked the western U.S., tramped in Tasmania and New Zealand, and trekked the mountains of Peru, my husband Ed and I are filled with awe and envy. Someday, given the time and stamina, we want to follow in her footsteps for some long-distance rambling in the United Kingdom.

But with only a single day to sample the trail that skirts England's entire southwestern extremity, our goal is far less lofty: Bus to the village of Zennor and walk back north along the Coast Path to our hotel in St.

Ives. The tourist office recommended this stretch of path because Cornwall's spotty off-season bus system services Zennor. The six-mile hiking distance sounded like an easy day for a couple of long-haul hikers—even for one with a weak knee like mine.

Our fellow traveler, who had just completed our planned route, doubts the six-mile estimate. "Maybe, as the crow flies," she says, "but it seemed much longer, and it took me five hours." She shakes her head at our cavalier, can-do attitude; she can see we are only a few miles behind her in age. "You do know this is supposed to be the most severe section of the entire South West Coast Path?"

*Most severe?* How did we miss *that* trail note? Suddenly, the bearer of this bad news does not seem so lovely, nor her smile so sweet. Could it be, in this ancient land of sorcerers and spirits, that we have met a crone, brewing "toil and trouble" for a couple of unsuspecting American hikers? Some mystery and mysticism would add to the day, *severe* conditions—not so much.

At Zennor the woman vanishes. We stand at the edge of the village under a leaden sky, pondering both the difficulties she has predicted and the practical matter of finding take-away for the trek. Zennor, a few winding lanes lined with dark and shuttered gray stone cottages, sleeps like it cannot face Monday. Either the villagers have left for work, or they are hiding behind closed doors.

Where are the children?

It is already 9 a.m. No one stirs in the churchyard cemetery either. Lichen-splotched Celtic crosses angle drunkenly out of the thick green sod marking ancient graves. The local Wayside Museum, set in a watermill, is locked up tight. Even The Tinners Arms pub and B&B, where D.H. Lawrence stayed briefly, is dark. We begin to despair we are in for a long and hungry hike, when the Zennor Chapel Guesthouse and Cafe opens to provision us for lunch.

The young waitress who serves us has never heard of the author of *Lady Chatterley's Lover*, but the cook admits Lawrence lived in nearby Tregethen. "It's a private house and they don't want visitors," she says, slapping a thick slab of margarine on our ham and tuna-mayo sandwiches for emphasis.

At 9:45 a.m., picnic in hand, we set off, feeling we have trespassed in Zennor long enough. The narrow road dwindles to a dirt path marked by a stone signpost announcing, "St. Ives, six miles." The broad Zennor Headland, crowned with a tumble of granite boulders, juts into the sea. A brass plaque commemorates the land's donation to the National Trust in 1953 by an enigmatic A.B. "In proud and happy memory of the friends whose love has sustained me."

And so we begin. One foot forward, then the other, and repeat. It's slow, but it is the way we choose to travel. We have done our share of clubbing and pubbing, but at this point in our lives, for a walk on the wild side we prefer just that, to travel by foot deep into the unsettled heart of a place. The whole of our life trajectory has arced this way, from years living in New York City, Brussels and Dallas to the present day, making our home on a quiet mountainside.

Now we tread on the very edge of England. To our right, the hills roll away to rounded summits where black granite *tors* erupt from the earth to break the smooth ridgeline. Nearly bare of trees, the hills are covered with a low impenetrable mix of blackberry brambles, thistles and scratchy bracken.

To our left, the land falls off. The Atlantic Ocean, unimpeded from Greenland, rolls in, changing color from navy to turquoise and roiling white. It bites into the coast, tearing off chunks of land and creating small boulder-strewn coves, high cliffs and gnarly headlands. We pass a woman with a camera to her face, who tells her companion, "I have to stop taking pictures of waves," and then compulsively clicks the shutter again.

This is the scenery we have come for, the land and sea that have haunted and inspired artists for centuries. For writers like Thomas Hardy and Daphne du Maurier, England's wild west—the lonely moors, *tors*, and jagged coastlines—were characters as carefully drawn as Eustacia Vye in Hardy's *Return of the Native* or the terrifying Joss Merlyn, proprietor of du Maurier's *Jamaica Inn*.

Hundreds, perhaps thousands of years of foot traffic have cut our path through the tough sod deep into the rocky earth. Long before the trail was absorbed into the South West Coast Path for tourists, the locals trod it to reach their pastures, fields and mines. We descend, and then climb sharply, using our hiking poles to steady ourselves on the rough terrain and rock outcroppings. Another descent, and we are slowed by boulders and bogs and slippery mud.

When moving, I can't lift my eyes from the uneven trail bed, so I have to stop to absorb my surroundings. The moors are green, yellow and purple depending on the play of sunlight and cloud shadows. High on the cliff, the wind gently ruffles our hair and brushes our cheeks, but on the ocean, we watch its rough squall whipping up white caps and driving the water into the shore.

All morning the heavy gray clouds threaten, but our luck holds, with just a few warning spits of rain. This country, hard-edged even on the brightest of days, presents serious dangers to a hiker during one of the region's frequent storms. At the base of Tregethen Cliff, the waves crash fifty feet into the air—and this on a relatively calm day. I imagine being caught between the angry sea and the wide, open hills, unprotected from the wind and the rain.

As we reach the top of a rise, we look inland toward a cluster of gray buildings—Tregethen. One house stands isolated high above the rest, next to an irregular stand of granite. Was this where Lawrence lived during World War I, in a structure visible far out to sea? If so, their war-

wary neighbors could be forgiven for suspecting the writer and his German wife—cousin of the enemy flying ace known as the Red Baron —chose it as a post from which to guide German boats that were terrorizing the coast.

A few other huddles of buildings, low farmhouses and barns, dot the distant countryside, too small to be called villages but large enough to assert a human presence across the broad, wild plateau. Tremedda. Wicca. Boscubben. Treveal. Trevalgan. Trowan. We tramp along to the staccato song we've created from the names of these ancient outposts.

For some 3000 years, the Cornish people have been laying out the patchwork of small green fields and pastures that our path skirts. The parcels are demarcated by indestructible hedges of local rock stacked in two parallel rows loaded with earth. These act like planters that nature, over time, fills to overflowing with tough native vegetation that can withstand the harsh weather on the moors. While impressed by the human ingenuity that has corralled some of the rugged land, we are awed that people have not been able to fetter nature's essential wildness.

At 12:30 p.m., a Coast Path marker shows we have come only three miles from Zennor. More disconcerting is the fact that the marker indicates 3.5 miles more to St. Ives. What kind of magic is this? Somehow the path has lengthened by a half mile since the first signpost in Zennor. The turn-off to Treveal tempts us, but we forge on, tackling yet another tough climb before settling in among the rocks to picnic at the top of Carn Naun Point.

"Severe?" I ask Ed as we lounge in the granite easy chairs nature has provided.

"Difficult at least," he admits, "but I only lost my balance twice."

Well, *that's* a relief. The piskies may tug at our ankles, but the mischievous fairies of Cornish folklore haven't tripped us up, yet. Unfortunately, there is still time, because we are less than halfway and getting tired.

We have come far enough to see the lighthouse that Virginia Woolf memorialized in her novel, which has been a beacon from our hotel window. However, St. Ives itself is still hidden by Pen Enys and Clodgy Points.

My weak knee, with a stab of pain, demands, *Are we there yet?*

We cross pastureland that dips perilously close to the cliffs. Modern barbed wire fences along the steep drop-offs supplement the ancient hedges. A sign marks the place where in 1950 twenty head of cattle crashed over the cliff and had to be hoisted back up—still alive and kicking. It seems to be a particularly eventful spot among all the twists and turns of the coastline. In 1941, the ship, *Bessemer City*, ran aground here, spewing its cargo of tinned food. The crew was saved and the cans that washed up on the rocks fed the locals for a long time. However, the labels washed off these gifts from the sea. No one knew if they'd be dining on corned beef—or sliced peaches.

At 2:15 p.m. another sign promises a one-and-a-half hour "stroll" the two remaining miles to St. Ives. I realize I'm hardly taking in the continuing beauty of the scenery because of the concentration it takes to keep my tired legs moving.

An hour later we crest Clodgy Point for a tantalizing vision of our destination, the golden crescent of Porthmeor Beach littered with surfers, the large hillside cemetery, the modernistic Tate St. Ives building, and the ancient Chapel of St. Nicholas crowning the hill at the far end of the town's peninsula. Like horses heading to the barn we speed up, but the path stretches on, rising and falling—endless. A signpost indicates yet one more mile, possibly the longest of the entire hike.

It's 4:15 p.m. Of course the trail ends; it always ends, one way or another. After solitary hours on a path where a few seabirds outnumbered the hikers, we arrive on the boardwalk of the municipal surfing beach, and a wave of ebullient vacationers crashes over us. There is a disconnect between this carefully raked slice of sand and bustling, sun-tanned humanity and the untamed coast so close at hand. Our muddy hiking gear and heavy boots are out of place among the bathing suits and flip-flops. Even the weather has been civilized, as if a sky-blue and gold bubble encases the town, protecting it from the lowering clouds that hovered over the trail.

Shucking our packs and a slight sense of disorientation, Ed and I settle in on the deck of the Porthmeor Cafe to fuel our urban re-entry with a platter of Cornish cheddar and a couple of pints of Sharp's Doom Bar amber lager. "Here's to the trail," we toast, "and to its ups and downs." Warmed by the sun, the alcohol and our success, we even hoist a glass to the woman/witch whose doubts could not deter us, even from conditions most severe.

Tony Farrell at Zennor Quoit

# ZENNOR QUOIT
*Tony Farrell*

Here, above the early field systems
And below the gaze of the nailed
Kestrel,

                the wind

       scatters

               clouds
         through the granite

                        uprights;

erodes         memories

                  and

      disperses us.

Detached.
We move amongst our lives;
Carrying the possibilities of what
Happened here.

As important as the
Burials within the chamber—
We are the continuing ritual around it.

The entrance to the Jamaica Inn

# CHEATER'S HIGH

*Laurie McAndish King*

Lying, cheating, and stealing are wrong—my parents taught me that. They never mentioned smuggling, though. And I never thought much about that particular enterprise until I visited Cornwall, where the people have been moving contraband for more than 800 years.

Curious about this questionable activity, I decided to visit the Smugglers Museum, which is situated in the Jamaica Inn, the very building that was central to Cornish writer Daphne du Maurier's eponymous psychological thriller. High winds, haunting fog and treacherous moors provide the backdrop for her tale of smuggling, thievery, murder and terror. The whole business had struck me as horrifying when I read the book. Once there, I hoped to learn more about what they called the "free trader" lifestyle—and the whole community's lifestyle.

En route, crossing the moor by bus, I had time to review what I knew. Cornish smuggling started in the twelfth century when locally produced tin began to be traded extensively throughout Europe for use in weaponry. Richard I levied a heavy tax on the valuable commodity, but impoverished miners could hardly afford to pay. Oppressive taxation —and thus smuggling—continued as subsequent rulers needed to fund various costly enterprises, including the One Hundred Years War, the Continental Wars, and the Napoleonic Wars.

By the late eighteenth century, the practice had swept the whole of Cornwall, as if carried by a relentless tide. Pretty much everyone participated: starving tinners, fisherman down on their luck, squires who liked their brandy, fishing boat owners making payments, gentlemen increasing their fortunes by ignoring midnight landings, retailers augmenting their incomes with under-the-counter sales, local men who were paid in drink for overnight use of their ponies—even government officials on the take. Poverty, oppressive taxes, and intractable tradition had combined to create a perfect storm.

Yet there is another aspect to smuggling, and du Maurier—who specialized in dark motives—understood it perfectly. "Desire to thwart the law is a basic human instinct ..." she wrote, "and the most honest of persons feels a tingle of pleasure if he succeeds, by some cunning means, in outwitting authority."

That tingle of pleasure has a name. It is known to psychologists as "cheater's high." Getting away with something by being clever provides a sense of accomplishment—a thrill, even. It asserts the individual's authority against a rigged system. And psychologists have found that it triggers built-in neurobiological rewards. This cheater's high seems to apply to everyone—even to people who expect to feel guilty from cheating—as long as there is no obvious victim. And in a poor and overtaxed land, the taxman hardly seems a victim. In fact, he is seen as the *cause* of smuggling, or "free trading," which is accepted as the natural and inevitable result of overzealous taxation.

No one likes the taxman—including me. With that thought in mind, I stepped into the museum where a sign at the entrance set the tone:

Pirate, Corsair, Smuggler, Freebooter, Contrabandist!

These are all romantic-sounding names conjuring up in the mind's eye stirring incidents from bygone times. But do not imagine for one minute that smugglers, like the swashbuckling pirates of the Spanish Main, are now just a part of history. The truth is that the smuggler is as active and daring today as he ever was in the past.

A rusty tin container labeled "Unecol Marshmallow" sat just inside the door. It had a false bottom. Using piles of puffy confectionary for smuggling struck me as implausible, and even silly. "They used *marshmallows* for smuggling?" I ventured vaguely, in the general direction of the man standing next to me.

"Mmm. They used every method available, and every man, too," he replied.

My new friend seemed to be something of an authority on smuggling, so I pressed for further details. "How many people did an average operation employ?"

"Well now, let's see." He closed his eyes and clasped his burly hands as if in prayer. "There would have been the men who kept watch from land—they tracked the position of government Preventive Men. And the spotsman, he was onboard and determined the point for landing. Beach access was best."

"How did they move the goods to shore?"

My friend opened his eyes again. "That was the lander's job; he mustered the muscle. The men had to work fast, and in the dark, so quite a few of 'em was needed. They might ha' used boats, or sometimes they just waded in if it was shallow."

I was getting a real education. "That sounds like a tough job."

"Yeah, but it's nothing like what the tubmen did. They was real athletes!"

"You said *tubmen?*"

"The tubman lugged two kegs tied together with a rope, one on his front and one on his back. He carried ninety pounds, and those kegs crushed the chest of more than one man. It was especially bad if they had to climb the cliffs—real athletes, they was. Of course they couldn't defend themselves, burdened down as they was with the kegs."

"I see—that would have been a problem."

"So that's where the batsmen come in."

"The batsmen."

"You know why they was called batsmen?"

"I'm sure you'll explain …"

"They carried the bats."

I smiled.

"Scores of 'em was needed. They'd line up with their bats, or with hand pistols, to make a protection line for the tubmen. They didn't mind usin' their weapons, either."

"It sounds dangerous."

"It was. But the wreckers was more so. You've seen the coastline around here?"

"I have. It's beautiful—very rugged."

"Very rugged is right, and we've always had lots of shipwrecks, which don't hurt us none."

"I imagine they hurt the sailors …"

"The sailors generally died, so it didn't bother them none, either, in the end." He paused. "You know how they died?"

I was beginning to get the picture.

"Some was drowned. The rest was killed by the wreckers."

I shot him a horrified look.

"See, the wreckers could legally claim any goods that washed t' shore. But it was illegal to claim any salvage if there was survivors."

I swallowed hard. "Are you saying … ?"

"I'm saying the survivors was condemned to death, and it was the law that did it."

So it was true. Predatory "wrecking" was a sinister aspect of the trade, just as du Maurier described it chillingly in *Jamaica Inn*. Locals profited so much from shipwrecks that they encouraged the process, often going as far as using lights to lure ships ashore at night, and murdering anyone who survived the shipwreck. Smuggling was a terrible business.

I proceeded slowly through the museum, absorbing its chilling displays. It seems there was almost nothing that could not be smuggled, and the methods for doing so were varied and ingenious. The cleverest—and most distressing—technique involved transporting live animals. Exotic birds were sedated and tied in silk stockings, then pinned into the smuggler's raincoat and walked across a border.

*The smuggler made the birds dead drunk by forcibly feeding them drops of alcohol. Their beaks were taped up to prevent them chirruping, should they come round too soon. Finches sold in Belgium for thirty pence would fetch seventy pence in Holland. A smuggler would carry anything from ten to twenty stockings at a time, with five birds to each stocking.*

I tried to picture a smuggler burdened with one hundred sedated finches stashed into silk stockings, nonchalantly crossing the border between Belgium and Holland. The birds would press against his body. He could not sit. One wrong move, one slip, one bumbling stranger's bump, would crush them. There was a fine line between life and death. He surely experienced cheater's high. The exhibit was disturbing. Disturbing, and a little bit exciting.

Another display explained in detail how to build a still for bootlegging—the first step in many smuggling careers. The headline was sensational:

£500 Every Week
Here is How it is Done!

Detailed instructions included a recommendation to keep the operation small to avoid arousing suspicion. I quickly calculated that £500/week is more than $40,000/year. If one doesn't pay taxes on that amount, it's the equivalent of $50,000—not bad for a small enterprise. Not a bad fit for a twenty-first-century writer looking for part-time work. I was warming to the concept and considered building my own still back at home. The construction looked easy. How hard can welding be? I took meticulous notes.

There were hollowed-out books and fruits, china figurines packed with opium, gunnysacks loaded with pearls, a French talcum powder canister fitted with a false bottom, and a stylish turban especially designed for smuggling hashish. A jaunty bag printed with "Export—Blue Mountain Ganja—Product of Jamaica" was displayed above a sign extolling the pleasures of that mirthful land:

*Ah, that sun-blessed beautiful island, set in a sea of azure blue, where music & laughter delight the ears, and the sweet soft gentle tang of marijuana smoke tantalizes the nostrils and soothes the weary worrying brain of man with dream thoughts of so many pleasures. Yes, in Jamaica one can openly purchase bags full of "the blessed weed" and walk away with it in a carrier like this.*

I felt a twinge of recognition. I may have carried a very small amount of the blessed weed across state borders a time or two myself (as I recall, a visit to the in-laws was involved). Did that make me a smuggler? My horror became tinged with intrigue.

One exhibit recommended the hollowed-out potato, a time-honored procedure and "still one of the best methods for making a smuggle." This seemed almost as laughable as the marshmallow-can stunt, and I began to imagine myself hiding contraband in potatoes and marshmallows. *Harmless*, I decided. *Completely harmless.*

Nearby, an elegant high-heeled sandal seduced from its spotlighted case. It appeared to offer no place for concealment—at first glance. But a slender glass vial had been secretly fitted into the heel, and "when filled with diamond chips ... produces large profits for the smuggler and a worthwhile fee for the attractive and disarming carrier." The sandal made smuggling seem glamorous. *I could be an attractive and disarming carrier*, I thought.

A corset caught my attention next. Along the inside of the top edge, short smudges marked the place it would have rubbed its wearer, just below the breast. Its secret pouch was easy to spot. I wondered how many carats this undergarment might conceal, and how many times it had been pressed into service. I imagined wearing the diamond-laden corset and sandals, and perhaps the stylish hashish-hiding turban as well. I could feel that cheater's high—*and I liked it.*

Leaving the museum, I found it easy enough to accept smuggling by impoverished miners forced to work in darkness, stooped over, often standing waist-deep in water. Some actually began to live underground rather than climbing rope ladders for hours every day to get to and from work. They were besieged by accidents, flooded tunnels and disease. Despair and near-starvation were facts of life. So was smuggling. Who could object?

But the rich smuggled, too. They favored luxury items over food. French brandy was one of the top movers; tobacco, china, silk and lace were also popular. Was smuggling wrong when the well-to-do engaged in the practice? I had to ask myself: Can one activity be acceptable or not, depending on who's doing it, or when, or why? From what I could tell, Cornwall did not seem to have suffered from its history of smuggling. Perhaps the citizens had reformed?

Climbing aboard the bus, I asked the driver whether the Cornish still move contraband these days. "Of course not," he replied heartily. "That's all in the past." Then quickly, under his breath he added, "What is it yer lookin' for, lass?"

Driving on the "wrong" side

# Driving Me Mad

*Anne Sigmon*

My friends and my husband had it all wrong: Driving on the wrong side of the road in England was easy; it was driving on the wrong side of the car that almost did me in.

From the moment I decided to join a group of friends on a week's sojourn to the Cornish peninsula, it was clear I'd need to rent a car. The closest England has to a wild west, Cornwall is about nature—the mists and bogs, the roiling sea, granite *tors*, ancient and mysterious stones tucked into backwoods corners. To see that Cornwall I'd need to get close; I'd need time to explore; I'd need wheels.

I had no encouragement.

"Forget it," one of my friends said. "I did it—once. Driving on the wrong side of the road … I was sure I was going to end up dead. I'd never do it again."

A second friend, fellow Cornwall traveler MJ, was keen to hike the notoriously slippery, granite-strewn trail around Zennor. Maryly planned to kayak the frigid and treacherous waters of the Atlantic. Yet everyone agreed that driving was too dangerous? I thought they were nuts.

After all, 35 percent of the world's population lives in countries, territories, possessions and protectorates that, like England, drive on the left. That's more than 2.3 billion people, from Anguilla to Zimbabwe. Come on, how hard could it be?

I invited my husband, Jack, to join me. I was sure he'd love the ancient sites I had in mind.

"Nooo. Nada."

"But why?"

"I don't want to drive on the left."

"Really?"

Given Jack's penchant for harebrained locomotion—whitewater canoeing, riding Mongolian horses bareback on the steppes, hunting grizzlies on foot in the Alaska wild—perhaps I should have taken note.

If Jack and my friends were so reluctant, why wasn't I? As a stroke patient taking high doses of blood thinner, I live with—and try not to be cowed by—the knowledge that even a minor accident could provoke a blood-drenched debacle.

I wasn't going to think about that. I'd never been afraid to drive; I wasn't going to start now.

Nonetheless, I thought, a wee bit of preparation might be prudent. An hour trolling the Internet for "tips on driving in England" reminded me that most cars in England are stick shifts (I've never driven a stick) and that relying on the free insurance offered by credit cards (my usual practice) might be chancy. English multi-lane roundabouts were described as "ingenious" but so tricky that migraine-inducing diagrams and umpteen YouTube videos were required to explain the "spider signs" and "exit strategies."

"It's handy to have a navigator to help you," one article advised. Did the author mean a GPS tracker? Or a human co-pilot? I'd be alone on the first—and longest—drive, when I'd rent a car in Exeter and motor 115 miles to St. Ives. As backup, shelling out three hundred dollars, I ordered a Garmin international GPS. Later, I discovered that the actual English maps were an add-on—another hundred bucks. And, since my unit arrived without an AC plug, I wouldn't be able to test it until I arrived in-country.

Perhaps computer simulation might prepare me? A free, on-line program forced me to "drive" using my computer's arrow keys. I was so clumsy with those up-down, left-right pulses that, even after two hours of practice, I never made it out of the virtual "parking lot" before "crashing." Fancier software like SimuRide and City Car wasn't compatible with my Macintosh setup. Several driving "games" required three-hundred-dollar consoles like Wii or Xbox.

I didn't have money or time for that nonsense. I'd just have to wing it. But I laid down four rules for myself:

- rent automatic transmission only
- pony up for all the insurance extras
- always use GPS
- ride with a companion whenever possible.

Simple! MJ and I would explore the area together once I joined the group in Cornwall, so I'd have a "human backup" for most of my wanderings.

Taxiing from Heathrow to my London hotel, I ignored the fog swirling around the tower of London, the boats on the Thames, the Georgian mansions of Marylebone. Instead, I sat behind the driver, watching his every maneuver, trying to imagine myself at the wheel, crossing traffic to turn right at lights, easing left into traffic circles, constantly checking both left and right for traffic and pedestrians. After an hour's ride, driving on the left seemed almost natural.

Easy peasy, I thought. I can do this.

Over lunch the next day, a London friend reminded me that, in Cornwall, I'd have to be prepared for the "lay-bys"—tiny pull-outs on the many one-track country lanes that are wide enough for one car only.

205

"The roads there are also rather hilly," she said. "Can be a bit of a squeeze."

Gulp.

From London, I hopped a train to Exeter, where I planned to rent the car the next day. But my driving exploit almost fizzled before I got anywhere near a rental car. Checking my paperwork, I discovered that my driver's license was missing, apparently snagged—and not returned, I suddenly remembered—by an overzealous desk clerk when I checked into my London hotel.

In a panic, I enlisted my Exeter hotel manager's help a in a frenzied round of phone calls—first to the concierge at my London hotel. She found the license. Then I called FedEx, UPS, the Royal Mail, and two courier services to see how to get it delivered to St. Ives. But the options to dispatch that three-inch piece of plastic the two hundred miles from London ranged from the impossible to the exorbitantly expensive. In the end, my only reasonable alternative was to hole up in Exeter for an extra day and wait for a FedEx special delivery. The cost: one hundred sixty dollars, one extra night in the hotel, and a hunk of pride.

A day and a half later, at Europcar's Exeter airport lot, I sank into the cockpit of my ride: a midnight blue Volkswagen Passat, a bit larger than I'd imagined (weren't Volkswagens supposed to be small?) but with the automatic transmission I'd demanded. I took my time, adjusted the seat and mirrors, tested the lights, the wipers. Not bad, despite the strange feel of the steering wheel on the right side of the car. The GPS needed time to charge, but I wasn't worried. My route was a straight shot down the A30 to St. Ives, only one turn required—the road to my group's lodging at Treganna Castle. I wouldn't need navigation for that.

I started the car, breathed in, pulled out. Maneuvering onto the airport ring road, I crossed the oncoming lanes, eased into the right turn, then felt a bump. Damn. I'd hit the curb. Already! I straightened the car and followed the sign toward the airport exit. Suddenly a maze of red construction cones rose up all over the road, crimson funnels directing traffic onto a freeway on-ramp in three directions around a gouged-out track of asphalt. M5, B183, A30. Quick, which way? There, left, over by the bank of ivy. As I tucked onto the ramp—WHACK! I heard a thud-scrape and felt a jolt just as the left rearview mirror flew out of its housing and swung by two thin wires, one white, the other pink. What did I hit? I looked back. Nothing but ivy. That's how I discovered that those quaint hedgerows lining Cornwall's narrow streets are really ancient granite walls prettied up with greenery.

Cars were coming up behind me. I had to move. The ramp channeled me into the center of a multi-lane freeway—the "M." I can't drive a hundred miles like this, with no mirror. I've got to pull over! The car drifted to the left again as if by osmosis. I corrected. A half dozen green directional signs loomed above. There! "Park n' Ride, 2 km." Ignoring everything else, I followed the signs through at least two route changes, clenching the wheel, drifting left and correcting right. Finally, the lot! I pulled in, stopped, breathed out. My medic-alert bracelet clinked as I slumped over the steering wheel. My inner voice whined, what a stupid, stupid idea, I'm going to kill myself.

All I wanted was to dump this beastly car, jump on a train, and never drive again. But first I'd have to return the car to the airport. Which way was it? I'd lost track. Then there'd be that damn red-cone gauntlet. And I'd have to find a train. I probably wouldn't reach St. Ives till midnight!

Or, I could buck up and drive the A30 like I'd planned. I sat up, shook off the panic. It was two-fifteen now. Even driving like an old grandma, I guessed I could reach St. Ives before dark.

I got out to inspect the car. A nasty white scrape, more than a foot long, marred the passenger-side door. Thank goodness for insurance! I grabbed the dangling mirror; it snapped back into place with, apparently, no harm done. I took it as a sign. I can do this.

At just that moment of decision, a Fiat mini-pickup pulled in beside me. A lanky guy—mid-thirties, I guessed—jumped down from the cab.

"Madam? I say, are you all right?"

What does he mean?

"I saw you weaving out there, followed you for a mile—thought maybe you needed help."

*God, he thinks I'm drunk.* I summoned my cheeriest, most sober tone. "Oh—no, I'm fine." I laughed. "Just a dumb American. My first time driving on the left. I think I've got the hang of it now." *Good thing he's not a cop!*

"You're sure?"

"I'm sure." Liar.

"I'll be off then. G'day."

Anxious to get going before I lost my nerve, I slid back into the Beast and followed the signs to A30 South, thankfully now past the construction. I settled into the slow lane and tried to keep my speed up to a respectable forty-five. My hands clutched the steering wheel. My eyes darted from the road to the rearview mirror, where I learned to gauge my position within the dashed lane markers reeling out behind me.

The roundabouts were one-eyed monsters, swirling vortices of peril. The Beast and I whirled through each spiral at grandma speed, clinging to the (thankfully marked) A30 lane. We were on a roll—until I missed the last exit at Hayle and shot out of the roundabout onto a snakelet of a track that was squished between two six-foot granite walls. Good lord! Is this road even wide enough for my car? Almost holding my breath, navigating by village signposts and a vague sense of direction, I somehow found my way to St. Ives Road. With no lane markers to guide me, I poked along—my palms sweaty, my back tense—scanning ahead for landmarks while trying to assess the perils of another wall scrape vs. a head-on smack. Suddenly, like a hidden sanctum emerging from the mist, there it was: the entrance to our castle abode.

Hi-fiving my friends inside, I had just one thought: Wine, now, and lots of it.

That first day was the worst. For the rest of the week, MJ sat to my left on "wall-woman" duty, piping, "Right! Move to the right!" each time we drifted toward a joust with granite. What is it about sitting on the right side of the car that transforms a left-standing wall into a magnet? I drove like a greenhorn, inching down zipper-thin lanes that couldn't accommodate two horses, much less two cars. I pinched into tiny by-way pullouts when traffic piled up behind us. Local drivers were endlessly patient—no honking or tailgating—just, I imagined, a few bemused chuckles. They knew.

The Garmin GPS was a bust, demanding precise street addresses when all we had were landmarks—tors, stone circles, tin mines. Laurie and Daphne joined us on our rambles and pitched in as old-school navigators using maps we bought in the local bookstore.

The magic of backwoods Cornwall was worth all the jittery angst of left-side driving. With the breeze at our backs, we watched lambs scuttle through a stone circle laid in 1500 BCE, felt salt on our faces as we stood on a cliff watching burly waves fling arcs of foam on yellow sand. The bruise-colored sky darkened to twilight as we tied wishing rags onto a Cloutie tree. We felt the power of hope as an 8000-year-old granite megalith turned golden in the setting sun.

Oh yes, it was worth it. I'm sure I'll return to Cornwall. I'll drive there again. But next time, I'll rent a Mini Cooper.

Tregenna Castle on the hillside

# Last Climb Up Tregenna Hill

*Joanna Biggar*

Out of synch, out of season, summer sun
on the summer sea. October, and I am
running up
for one forgotten thing
I still cannot remember.
Was it my words?
Fern paths, palm trees, golf grass green
as winter in a greedy land,
I pause, wanting breath,
wanting what I have come for
up this stony path.
But my companions are not here.
Gone as ghosts, the writers,
the breeze wiped clean of their
laughter, their stories, their laments.
Gone Linda beneath the faded lamplight
in the cottage of the weeping stone.
Gone myself.
Inside the stone-walled castle,

wedding revelers dance,
but I am not invited.
Now a stranger here,
I look only for what is lost.
The wind strikes noon;
My blood turns.
Alone
in this moment,
I freeze in the sun
and fear
that,
on the great mossy green,
without
what I have come for,
I will become
the last stone standing.

# AUTHOR BIOGRAPHIES

**Unity Barry** graduated from the San Francisco Art Institute, but after she worked for way too long in the corporate world, she retired to write about her favorite subjects—artists and Paris during the Gilded Age. She recently finished her first historical novel, *Luminous—Berthe Morisot and the Birth of Impressionism* and is starting her next about Mary Cassatt. Unity was a short-listed finalist in the 2011 William Faulkner-William Wisdom Writing Competition and has two pieces in the anthology *Wandering Paris: Luminaries and Love in the City of Light.*

**Daphne Beyers** grew up near Amish country in northeastern Pennsylvania, often finding herself caught in traffic behind wheel and buggy carriages. She's lived many places including London, New York City, San Francisco, Berkeley, and Palm Springs. Daphne taught herself to program at the age of thirteen and works as a computer consultant for various Fortune 500 companies in the Bay Area. Her first essay, "Existential Cafe,"was published in an award-winning anthology of Parisian stories, *Wandering in Paris: Luminaries and Love in the City of Light.* She currently lives north of San Francisco with a Scottish Terrier who thinks he's a dragon.

**Sandra Bracken** made the first of many journeys alone to Peru where she walked the hills around Sacsayhuaman, photographed the stonework there and chartered a plane to fly over the lines at Nazca—all in the pursuit of art. She has a master's degree in fine arts, taught drawing for twenty years and has exhibited sculpture and drawings in galleries and museums in the U.S. She collaborated on a collection of poems and collages, *Meet Me at the Wayside Body Shop* and produced a chapbook of poems, *New Moon*. Sandra's travel stories were included in *Venturing in Ireland: Quest for the Modern Celtic Soul* and *Venturing in Italy: Puglia, land between two seas* and *Wandering in Paris: Luminaries and Love in the City of Light*. Sandra lives in Maryland near her three children and five grandchildren. Her most recent travels have been with her husband —in pursuit of fish.

As the French child of a Jewish mother, **Antoinette Constable** witnessed atrocities inflicted on relatives, friends and strangers in Nazi-occupied France during WWII. She used this material to compile a chapbook of war-related poems, *The Lasting War*, published in December 2014. Antoinette has published numerous poems, four chapters of a novel, and prose pieces unrelated to the war. She's won a first poetry prize from PEN, an Ann Stanford award from SCA University, a month-long stay at a prestigious writers' retreat at Mesa Refuge in Point Reyes Station, California, and has contributed to the award-winning Wanderland Writers anthology, *Wandering in Paris: Luminaries and Love in the City of Light*. One of her poems served as inspiration for a Charleston Black Theatre production. Antoinette suffers headaches from not reading enough, enjoys puns, great food and friends, though not necessarily in this order.

**Tony Farrell** is a St. Ives man whose family has been involved for generations in fishing, seafaring and mining. He went to sea for a time after leaving school and before going to university. He has a BA Honours degree in English and in archaeology and did post-graduate research in archaeology at The Queen's University of Belfast. Tony has taught, and lectured, in further and higher education, and for nearly twenty years he was the Head of English at St. Ives School. He has also worked as a nautical archaeologist at the National Maritime Museum, Greenwich. Tony has published research papers in leading archaeological and historical journals and has published a poetry textbook. He has an intimate knowledge of St. Ives and the moors of West Penwith.

**Thomas Harrell** has joined the ranks of former lawyers who became writers. After sixteen years working for a Wall Street firm, the last six on dialysis, he received a new kidney eight years ago. With this second chance, he decided to leave the law and pursue two of his life passions: travel and writing. He has traveled to numerous countries, although not nearly enough yet. He has written about travel in several of these countries, including Argentina, Bosnia, China, and Italy. He also writes personal essays, many set in the South, where he was raised. Tom studied history and politics in college and is writing a spy novel set during the Civil War. He lives in San Francisco, California.

**Kitty Hughes** grew up in Arkansas and now lives in Oakland, California, with an ongoing interest in sense of place. She has conducted two research projects on local ethnic history—the most recent, "the Swedish History of the East Bay," funded by a grant from the Bernard Osher Pro Suecia Foundation. In 2014, she was a writer in residence at the Writers Colony at Dairy Hollow in Eureka Springs in the Arkansas Ozarks. Her novel-in-progress *Rendezvous* was named as a semi-finalist in the William Faulkner-William Wisdom Writing Competition. Kitty has published in several collections, including an anthology titled *Wondrous Child* (North Atlantic Press). She published an essay on Gertrude Stein, an underappreciated Oaklander, in *Wandering in Paris* and has given local tours of sites associated with the Stein family in Oakland.

**Laurie McAndish King** hardly ever feels Cheater's High—but when she does, she loves it. Her book of travel stories, *Lost, Kidnapped, Eaten Alive! True Stories from a Curious Traveler*, was published in 2014. Laurie's award-winning essays and photography have appeared in *Smithsonian* magazine, the *San Francisco Chronicle*, Travelers' Tales' *The Best Women's Travel Writing*, *The Sun* literary journal, and other magazines and literary anthologies. Her mobile app about the San Francisco Waterfront is 5-star rated in the Apple iTunes store. Laurie also wrote *An Erotic Alphabet* and co-edited, along with Linda Watanabe McFerrin, two volumes of erotica in the *Hot Flashes, sexy little stories & poems* series. She has an undergraduate degree in philosophy and a master's degree in education. Laurie lives in northern California. www.LaurieMcAndishKing.com

**Ethel Mussen** is a doughty nonagenarian who lives high on a hill above Berkeley and enjoys the wide-eyed enthusiasm of the Wanderland travelers as they hunker down in off-beat places to explore the world. Fifty years in providing health care of various sorts—the last 35 in teaching about and treating speech and hearing disorders—honed her anthropological approach to people and customs. A collector's interest in potters and their ceramics offered an additional slant in production and business of local craftsmen. Repeated spells of living in New Zealand, France and

Italy gave more insight into the effects and variety of cultural assumptions in local politics, business and behavior. These experiences and interests bias Ethel's emotional and scholarly response to the beauty and strangeness of each new voyage. Her late husband, Paul, used to regale her and their two children with the assurance that with every discovery, good or bad, "This is a cultural experience!" She utters that mantra with each new trip.

**Mary Jean Pramik**, a coalminer's daughter and a great, great-granddaughter of the Mongolian plain, has hitch-hiked across the United States, tracked May apples in Ohio, chased children through wet mountains of California, fended off bill collectors in tropical San Francisco, and counted sharp-taloned bird carcasses along the Pacific's Point Reyes sands. Communicating with screeching penguin hoards in Antarctica remains a high point of her sojourn on this planet. MJ earned undergraduate and graduate degrees in biological sciences, and completed an MFA in writing. She moonlights as a medical writer, penning such scientific thrillers as *Norenthindrone, The First Three Decades*, the fast-paced history of the first birth control pill extracted from a Mexican yam. Winner of the coveted Mary Womer Medal and a Travelers' Tales Solis Award, MJ's articles and essays have appeared in *Nature Biotechnology, Drug Topics,* and *Cosmetic Surgery News*, and mainstream publications such as *Good Housekeeping, Odyssey*, and the *National Enquirer.* She has contributed to the "*Venturing in*" travel series on the Canal du Midi, Southern Greece, Southern Ireland, and Puglia, Italy, and the "*Wandering in*" series for Costa Rica and Bali. MJ teaches graduate writing skills in the College of Science and Engineering at San Francisco State University.

**Lynne Rutan** isn't sure whether it was in the marbled luxury of San Francisco's Fairmont Hotel or amid the natural splendor of the Grand Tetons, but somewhere during a cross-country trip with her grandparents when she was thirteen, the travel bug bit— hard—and she's still scratching the itch four decades later. While living in New York City she worked all over the world for the American Society of Travel Agents and other travel industry companies and freelanced for travel trade magazines and the *New York Daily News*. Six years in Brussels gave her the opportunity to explore Europe and fueled her passion for cooking and culinary tourism. Lynne discovered another passion, hiking, during a four-day adventure to Machu Picchu and has since trekked in Tasmania, New Zealand, Tibet, Canada and the mountains that surround her home in Park City, Utah.

**Anne Sigmon** flunked jump rope in seventh grade and washed out of college PE. After college, she headed for San Francisco and a career in public relations. Exotic travel was the stuff of dreams until, at 38, she married Jack, took tea with erstwhile headhunters in Borneo and climbed Mt. Kilimanjaro at 43. Five years later, she was zapped by a career-ending stroke caused by an obscure autoimmune disease called Antiphospholipid Syndrome (APS). She may be stuck with blood thinners and a damaged brain, but she's still traveling to isolated regions ranging from Botswana to Burma and, most recently, to Syria, Jordan, and a remote rainforest in Costa Rica. Anne's personal essays and travel stories have appeared in local and national publications including *Good Housekeeping* and *Stroke Connection* magazines and the anthologies *Wandering in Costa Rica*, *Chicken Soup for the Soul: Find Your Happiness*, and *Travel Stories from Around the Globe*. She is currently working on a memoir about her experience with stroke and autoimmune disease. Anne's blog www.JunglePants.com offers travel tales and tips about adventure travel off the beaten path. On her author website, www.AnneSigmon.com, she writes about—and offers tips on—living with stroke and autoimmune disease.

**Maryly Snow** is an Oakland-born visual artist once known for her 1979 installation *An Act of Bad Taste By a Woman Raised for Impeccability.* This garnered her Warholian fifteen minutes of fame via a news clip on a local San Francisco television station and an invitation to appear on *Good Morning America.* These days she is primarily a printmaker with etchings in the Library of Congress, the Fine Arts Museum of San Francisco, the University of California, Berkeley, and many corporate and private collections. As an art and architecture visual librarian at UC Berkeley (remember 35mm slides?) before she retired in 2007, Maryly published many papers, winning the Nancy DeLaurier Writing Award in 2000 for her briefly titled essay *Pedagogical Consequences of Photomechanical Reproduction in the Visual Histories: From Copy Photography to Digital Mnemonics* (in Visual Resources 12:3-4, 1996 (double issue entitled, *Copyright, Fair Use and the Great Image Debate*). More recently, she was the editor of the award-winning book *California Society of Printmakers: One Hundred Years, 1913-2013,* currently undergoing conversion to an e-book. Maryly's West Oakland studio is open by appointment. www.snowstudios.com

# EDITOR BIOGRAPHIES

**Joanna Biggar** is a teacher, writer and traveler whose special places of the heart include the California coast and the South of France. She has degrees in Chinese and French and, as a professional writer for twenty-five years, has written poetry, fiction, personal essays, features, news and travel articles for hundreds of publications including *The Washington Post Magazine, Psychology Today, The International Herald Tribune,* and *The Wall Street Journal.* Her book *Travels and Other Poems* was published in 1996, and her most recent travel essays have appeared in the Venturing series, whose anthologies include books on France, Greece, Ireland, Italy and Costa Rica. A novel, *That Paris Year,* was published by Alan Squire Publishing in 2010.

Joanna has taught journalism, creative writing, personal essay and travel writing since 1984 in many venues and serves as a judge for best journalism awards for the Northern California Society of Professional Journalists. She has also taught reading and writing at St. Martin de Porres Middle School and Emiliano Zapata Street Academy in Oakland, California, where she makes her home. For the last year she has been writing and doing research for upcoming work in Aix-en-Provence, France. Contact Joanna through email (jobiggar@gmail.com), Facebook at That Paris Year, or her blog, www.joannabiggar.org.

**Linda Watanabe McFerrin** (www.lwmcferrin.com) is a poet, travel writer, novelist and contributor to numerous newspapers, magazines and anthologies. She is the author of two poetry collections, past editor of a popular Northern California guidebook and a winner of the Katherine Anne Porter Prize for Fiction. Her novel, *Namako: Sea Cucumber*, was named Best Book for the Teen-Age by the New York Public Library. In addition to authoring an award-winning short story collection, *The Hand of Buddha*, she has co-edited twelve anthologies, including the *Hot Flashes: sexy little stories & poems* series. Her latest novel, *Dead Love* (Stone Bridge Press, 2009), was short-listed as a finalist in the 2007 William Faulkner-William Wisdom Creative Competition and was a Bram Stoker Award Finalist for Superior Achievement in a Novel.

Linda has judged the San Francisco Literary Awards, the Josephine Miles Award for Literary Excellence and the Kiriyama Prize, served as a visiting mentor for the Loft Mentor Series and been guest faculty at the Oklahoma Arts Institute. A past NEA Panelist and juror for the Marin Literary Arts Council and the founder of Left Coast Writers®, she has led workshops in Greece, France, Italy, Ireland, England, Central America, Indonesia, Spain and the United States and has mentored a long list of accomplished writers and best-selling authors toward publication.